Creative Analysis

Creative Analysis: Art, creativity and clinical process explores the dynamics of creativity in psychoanalytic treatment. It argues that the creative process of the analytic interaction is characterized by specific forms of feeling, thinking and, most importantly, relating that result in the emergence of something new – therapeutic change. The artistic aspects of psychoanalysis and various features of creativity in analytic treatment are explored. Clinical examples are discussed at length.

George Hagman presents a new model of the psychology of creativity and art that helps us to better understand the clinical process. The book explores and develops several important implications of Hagman's main thesis: the psychodynamics of art, the creativity of the brain, aesthetic aspects of the treatment relationship, and the creativity of the analyst and analysand.

Change in analysis is driven not just by the analyst's interventions but also by the patient's own motivation and capacity for self-transformation. This change is depicted here as an in-depth psychological process that explores the sources of the patient's resistance to self-actualization and identifies hidden potential, unrealized capacities and strengths. *Creative Analysis: Art, creativity and clinical process* reformulates psychoanalytic therapy as a form of art that can help patients realize their potential, which may have been blocked, inhibited, denied or derailed. The book will be of interest to psychoanalysts, psychotherapists, graduates and students, including the educated public interested in art.

George Hagman is a psychoanalyst and clinical social worker practicing in New York City and Connecticut. He is a member of the faculty of the National Psychological Association for Psychoanalysis and the author of *The Artist's Mind: A psychoanalytic perspective on creativity, modern art and modern artists*, published by Routledge, 2010.

PSYCHOANALYTIC INQUIRY BOOK SERIES
JOSEPH D. LICHTENBERG
SERIES EDITOR

Like its counterpart, *Psychoanalytic Inquiry: A Topical Journal for Mental Health Professionals*, the Psychoanalytic Inquiry Book Series presents a diversity of subjects within a diversity of approaches to those subjects. Under the editorship of Joseph Lichtenberg, in collaboration with Melvin Bornstein and the editorial board of *Psychoanalytic Inquiry*, the volumes in this series strike a balance between research, theory, and clinical application. We are honored to have published the works of various innovators in psychoanalysis, such as Frank Lachmann, James Fosshage, Robert Stolorow, Donna Orange, Louis Sander, Léon Wurmser, James Grotstein, Joseph Jones, Doris Brothers, Fredric Busch, and Joseph Lichtenberg, among others.

The series includes books and monographs on mainline psychoanalytic topics, such as sexuality, narcissism, trauma, homosexuality, jealousy, envy, and varied aspects of analytic process and technique. In our efforts to broaden the field of analytic interest, the series has incorporated and embraced innovative discoveries in infant research, self psychology, intersubjectivity, motivational systems, affects as process, responses to cancer, borderline states, contextualism, postmodernism, attachment research and theory, medication, and mentalization. As further investigations in psychoanalysis come to fruition, we seek to present them in readable, easily comprehensible writing.

After 25 years, the core vision of this series remains the investigation, analysis and discussion of developments on the cutting edge of the psychoanalytic field, inspired by a boundless spirit of inquiry.

PSYCHOANALYTIC INQUIRY BOOK SERIES
JOSEPH D. LICHTENBERG
SERIES EDITOR

Vol. 45
Creative Analysis: Art, Creativity and Clinical Process
George Hagman

Vol. 44
The Search for a Relational Home: An Intersubjective View of Therapeutic Action
Chris Jaenicke

Vol. 43
Structures of Subjectivity: Explorations in Psychoanalytic Phenomenology and Contextualism, 2nd Edition
George E. Atwood and Robert D. Stolorow

Vol. 42
Psychoanalytic Complexity: Clinical Attitudes for Therapeutic Change
William J. Coburn

Vol. 41
Metaphor and Fields: Common Ground, Common Language and the Future of Psychoanalysis
S. Montana Katz (ed)

Vol. 40
Growth and Turbulence in the Container/Contained: Bion's Continuing Legacy
Howard B. Levine & Lawrence J. Brown (eds.)

Vol. 39
Nothing Good Is Allowed to Stand: An Integrative View of the Negative Therapeutic Reaction
Léon Wurmser & Heidrun Jarass (eds.)

Vol. 38
Self Experiences in Group, Revisited: Affective Attachments, Intersubjective Regulations, and Human Understanding
Irene Harwood, Walter Stone, & Malcolm Pines (eds.)

Vol. 37
The Abyss of Madness
George E. Atwood

Vol. 36
Manual of Panic Focused Psychodynamic Psychotherapy – eXtended Range
Fredric N. Busch, Barbara L. Milrod, Meriamne B. Singer, & Andrew C. Aronson

Vol. 35
World, Affectivity, Trauma: Heidegger and Post-Cartesian Psychoanalysis
Robert D. Stolorow

Vol. 34
Change in Psychoanalysis: An Analyst's Reflections on the Therapeutic Relationship
Chris Jaenicke

Vol. 33
Psychoanalysis and Motivational Systems: A New Look
Joseph D. Lichtenberg, Frank M. Lachmann, & James L. Fosshage

Vol. 32
Persons in Context: The Challenge of Individuality in Theory and Practice
Roger Frie & William J. Coburn (eds.)

Vol. 31
Toward an Emancipatory Psychoanalysis: Brandchaft's Intersubjective Vision
Bernard Brandchaft, Shelley Doctors, & Dorienne Sorter

Vol. 30
From Psychoanalytic Narrative to Empirical Single Case Research: Implications for Psychoanalytic Practice
Horst Kächele, Joseph Schachter, Helmut Thomä & the Ulm Psychoanalytic Process Research Study Group

Vol. 29
Mentalization: Theoretical Considerations, Research Findings, and Clinical Implications
Fredric N. Busch (ed.)

Vol. 28
Transforming Narcissism: Reflections on Empathy, Humor, and Expectations
Frank M. Lachmann

Vol. 27
Toward a Psychology of Uncertainty: Trauma-Centered Psychoanalysis
Doris Brothers

Vol. 26
Living Systems, Evolving Consciousness, and the Emerging Person: A Selection of Papers from the Life Work of Louis Sander
Gherardo Amadei & Ilaria Bianchi (eds.)

Vol. 25
Sensuality and Sexuality across the Divide of Shame
Joseph D. Lichtenberg

Vol. 24
Jealousy and Envy: New Views about Two Powerful Feelings
Léon Wurmser & Heidrun Jarass (eds.)

Vol. 23
Trauma and Human Existence: Autobiographical, Psychoanalytic, and Philosophical Reflections
Robert D. Stolorow

To my wonderful sister Ann Marie Cardinal

Creative Analysis

Art, creativity and clinical process

George Hagman

Routledge
Taylor & Francis Group
LONDON AND NEW YORK

First published 2015
by Routledge
4 Park Square, Milton Park, Abingdon, Oxon OX14 4RN
605 Third Avenue, New York, NY 10017

Routledge is an imprint of the Taylor & Francis Group, an informa business

British Library Cataloguing in Publication Data
A catalogue record for this book is available from the British Library

Library of Congress Cataloging-in-Publication Data
Hagman, George.
Creative analysis : art, creativity, and clinical process / George Hagman.
pages cm. — (Psychoanalytic inquiry book series ; Vol. 45)
ISBN 978-0-415-69626-5 — ISBN 978-0-415-69627-2
1. Psychoanalysis and art. I. Title.
N72.P74H34 2014
701'.15—dc23

2014022494

ISBN: 978-0-415-69626-5 (hbk)
ISBN: 978-0-415-69627-2 (pbk)
ISBN: 978-1-315-73969-4 (ebk)

Typeset in Times New Roman
by RefineCatch Limited, Bungay, Suffolk

Contents

Preface

In this book I propose a definition of Art and artistic creativity, and I explore the implications of the definition for psychoanalytic therapy. I hope that the notion that psychoanalysis is an art form and that a form of artistic creativity is at the heart of the analytic process are helpful to the reader. The book is not about art therapy, nor the use of art therapy techniques in analysis. It is not about the "art" of psychoanalysis – the non-rational, implicit, spontaneous and personalizing aspects of analytic technique, in other words the analyst's style – although I will touch on all these issues from time to time. By starting with a specific definition of art, I engage in a rigorous investigation of psychoanalysis as an art form. The reader will decide for her- or himself whether I have succeeded, and whether the ideas are useful. I hope they are.

I have been in training as an artist, working (for a time in my youth) as an artist, enjoying art, thinking about art, writing about art or talking with people about art for half a century. I gave up my ambitions to be an artist many years ago, and chose to become a social worker and analyst; but my interest in art has never flagged. During my analytic training, I became interested in the application of Winnicott's ideas to creativity and art. The insights provided by his paper "The use of an object" into the process of creation/discovery of something "new" is still the well-spring for most of my ideas.

Years later, I decided (one fateful day on my analyst's couch) to write a paper which applied Self Psychology to the creative process. That paper (Hagman, 2000) opened up a world of ideas to me. From that point I continued to study the question of aesthetic experience in general, and specifically, Beauty, Ugliness, and the Sublime. These papers were the core of my first book *Aesthetic Experience: Beauty, Creativity and the Search for the Ideal* published by Rodopi Press in 2006. Along the way I became friends with Carl Rotenberg, M.D., whose writings and friendship fueled my first writings (and led to our co-editing a volume in Joe Lichtenberg's journal, *Psychoanalytic Inquiry*), and Carol M. Press, Ed.D, a choreographer, dancer and scholar, who has supported and worked with me for many years. Carl and Carol were my companions during those initial years of study, lecturing and writing.

That first book was mostly theoretical, but also during those years Carol and I began to conduct workshops at various conferences, and I began to write and talk about how our ideas could be applied to the psychology of artists and the evolution of modern art. Gradually I had the core material for my second book in which I further explored the creative process using an analytic lens and showed how this perspective could illuminate the dynamics of creative artists and the development of modern art during the twentieth century (Hagman 2010a). During the writing of that book I studied the art of Marcel Duchamp and Andy Warhol (among others). Both of these important artists challenged traditional definitions of art, and provoked me to rethink my assumptions.

I had known for some time that the definition of art was one of the most important problems of aesthetics, art criticism and cultures. However, in regards to psychoanalysis I observed that most analysts who studied art and artists utilized vague definitions which were largely derived from romantic, late nineteenth- and early twentieth-century aesthetic values. Of course, psychoanalysis had its own part to play in the evolution of modern aesthetics, so the influence was mutual and important. The problem is that much psychoanalytic thinking about art is western centered and limited by a romantic notion of the artistic hero, working in isolation and wresting artistic imagery from the unconscious – or some derivative of that myth. However, over time, I have become influenced by the writing of Ellen Dissanayake, a scholar and friend of psychoanalysis, who argued that any definition of art had to apply to all of the arts, across culture and historical time. All of this forced me to consider what art "is", ontologically speaking. In an attempt to explain this I wrote the first chapter of this book. There you will read that the essence of art is its psychological nature. Art "is" not a thing, an activity or a cultural institution, it is a fundamental way in which we engage with the world, and in particular, how we engage with and affect our own subjectivity, in all three of its dimensions: cultural, relational and personal. Through Art human subjectivity becomes objectified, perfected and re-internalized in an unending process of psychological refinement. I do not mean this in a Hegelian sense – there is no upward trajectory to this process over time. Rather it is a protean flux of refinement, disruption and continual change, which reflects the nature of our social experience, our relationships with others and our own inner sense of self. Art has no fixed goal and no standard formal structure, but it is one of the primary ways we discover who we are, and through which we create and elaborate our subjective lives. This first chapter is not clinical, but I ask for the reader's patience since it provides the theoretical rationale for the chapters that follow. It is necessary to expand the definition of what art is in order to appreciate my arguments regarding psychoanalysis as an art form.

Almost inevitably I was led to consider the relation between this psychological definition of art and psychoanalysis, my daily work. To my surprise I found that my model of Art mapped quite well onto recent models of psychoanalytic practice. In particular, the ideas of intersubjectivity, self psychology, neuropsychological research, infant research and complexity. So with this rich set of psychoanalytic ideas in the background I began to put together this book. Thus you will find in here a chapter on psychoanalysis as an art form, as well as some supporting evidence from brain research regarding the inherent creative capacity of the brain. The next chapter (co-written with Carol Press) looks at implicit relational aspects of right brain communication as an aesthetic experience of interaction. Then we shift our focus to the creativity of the analyst and the creativity of analysand in paired chapters in which we consider the separate aspects of the analytic relationship. An integrative chapter follows on the complex nature of Creative Analysis, using an extended case history by way of illustration. The book closes with a short reflection on the nature of creative living, a lovely Winnicottian concept.

Although I believe that I am primarily a self-psychologist, you will see that I move flexibly among models when the evidence compels me. My problem here was to define art and then to think about psychoanalysis as an art-form. Accomplishing this goal required that I search my theoretical and clinical toolbox for anything that seemed right for the problem. The end result is a somewhat mixed model; however, I think for most people nowadays this is no longer a big issue.

Although I tend to keep the writing to myself I must thank a few people. First there is Carol M. Press, Ed.D, my sometime co-author and inspiration. Her friendship has been a source of strength and ideas for many years. In addition, still, the memory of Carl Rotenberg, colleague and friend. Joe Lichtenberg, M.D., for his support in the self-psychology community and his offer to write the preface as well as to include this book in his excellent *Psychoanalytic Inquiry* series. There are many others: Karen Schwartz, Leslie Hogan, David Shaddock (all of whom shared a wonderful trip to Umbria with Carol and myself to present at the Spoleto Festival of the Arts in 2012); my friend, analyst and photographer Linda Cummings; Ellen Dissanayake whose research into the intimate sources of aesthetics and art inspired and guided me, and whose availability and critical eye improved my thinking and writing; Anna and Paul Orenstein; Kate Hawes, my editor at Routledge, for her support, enthusiasm and patience; and Rosemary Balsam for asking me to write the reviews, which led to Chapters 3 and 8. I also want to thank several individuals and organizations who invited me to give talks or workshops about various aspects of this book. They are: the International Association for Psychoanalytic Self Psychology; the Connecticut Society for Psychoanalytic Psychology; the American Society for Psychoanalysis in Clinical Social Work; the International Psychoanalytic Association; Francesco Castellet y Ballara and Claudia Spadazzi of the Italian Psychoanalytic Society and the Spoleto Festival of the Arts; Barry Panter at Creativity and Madness, Santa Fe; Sharon Nuewald and the Oklahoma Psychoanalytic Society; and Sandra Indig and the New York Chapter of the NYS Society for Clinical Social Work.

Finally, I want to thank my son Peter and daughter Elena, for the joy they give me.

And Moira, for her love, patience and acceptance.

Several of the chapters in this book have appeared in somewhat different forms in other publications.

Chapters 3 and 8 are expanded modifications of three book reviews which I wrote for the *Journal of the American Psychoanalytic Association* in Volume 61, 2013 and Volume 62, 2014. In those articles I reviewed "The Science and Art of Psychotherapy" by Allen Schore, "The Master and His Emissary" by lan McGilchrist, and "The Creating Psyche: Theory and Practice of Teriatry Processes" by Hector Fiorinni. I want to thank SAGE publications for permission to use material from those essays.

Chapter 4 is a slightly edited version of a paper which I co-wrote with Carol Press, titled "Between aesthetics, the coconstruction of empathy, and the clinical", which was published in *Psychoanalytic Inquiry*, under the general editorship of Joseph Lichtenberg, M.D. The issue was titled *Forms of Creative Expression in Psychoanalysis.* and edited by Carol with Roz and Alan Kindler.

Chapter 5 was published in 2008 under the title "The creative analyst: How art can inform clinical practice" in Volume 4, issue 1 of the *International Journal of Psychoanalytic Self Psychology* under the general editorship of William Coburn, Ph.D.

Chapter 1

What art is

In this chapter, I will define Art as the *psychological processes* involved in art creation and appreciation. This is not to say that the art object is not important, but the defining element is the psychological work that the artist engages in as he creates the artwork. Whenever this particular psychological process is engaged in, there is art.

Once we separate out the definition of art from the cultural institutions and products which we associated with art we will find that psychoanalysis, is a form of art, a process in which subjectivity is externalized, worked on and perfected. In this case creativity is at the heart of the analytic enterprise and process. So in this chapter we will look anew at art. I will propose a definition which is very specific, but also highly generalizable to areas of human life and action beyond the cultural activities and products which we have traditionally defined as art. As we will see in the next chapter, one of these art forms is psychoanalysis itself.

Classical psychoanalysts never considered what art is. Freud appeared to view art as a form of defensive behavior, which he saw as an effective opportunity for the mobilization of a range of different psychological mechanisms, such as displacement, condensation, and most importantly, sublimation. Despite the interest Freud showed in art throughout his writings, in the end he saw art as an ancillary phenomenon, not basic or essential to human psychological life. Of course at the time, the notion of a drive to create art would have been out of keeping with the sexual and aggressive instinct model. Art was an epiphenomenon, one of many strategies available to human beings to channel their disruptive instincts into safe channels.

This chapter argues that the creation of art and the valuing of art is a fundamental human need. In agreement with recent scholarship in evolutionary theory, neurobiology, and cultural studies (see the appendix for a review of this research), I believe that the drive to create and value art developed within human communities during the Prehistoric age and continued to be elaborated into modern times (Dissanayake, 2009, pp. 153–154). In addition, art had an adaptive function in early human communities and its importance is linked to basic elements in attachment and self-experience. Art helped communities be more cohesive and therefore more viable. Individuals developed an instinct for art because the function of art in human life increased the probability of survival, both for the individual and the society within which he lived and worked.

Before proceeding further let me make a point about my terminology. I am distinguishing the term "art" from the more general definition of the cultural institution as well as the general class of products referred to as art. I will be discussing art as a unique type of psychological process which results in artworks, and which is valued by all cultures and referred to under the general term Art. I also distinguish art from aesthetic experience, which is a more general term for the human tendency to organize experience into formal structures and patterns that are valued and appreciated. Aesthetic experiences such as beauty, ugliness and the sublime play an important role in many forms of art. However, though aesthetics is important to art (as it is important to human experience more generally, though normally less obviously) it does not define it.

In the next section I will review the psychoanalytic literature regarding the nature of art. I have selected representative writings, which best capture analysts's thinking on what art "is". Not surprisingly we will see how analysts have emphasized the psychological processes involved. My goal, however, will be to differentiate the unique or distinctive psychological nature of art which distinguishes it from other psychological phenomena. Following this review I will offer and elaborate on a comprehensive, integrative definition of art that will serve as the theoretical foundation of our exploration of creative psychoanalysis.

Psychoanalytic approaches to art

Since Freud's first important papers on art and creativity (1908, 1910) psychoanalysts have worked to understand the nature of art, aesthetic experience and creativity.

In his paper "Creative writers and day-dreaming" (1908) Freud understood adult creativity as an extension and elaboration of the psychological activity of daydreaming. Since daydreaming often involves forbidden or otherwise disturbing wish fulfillments, the daydreamer usually keeps them to himself. However, the artist engages in creative work, which being the adult equivalent of childhood play, allows for the expression of Phantasy in a disguised fashion that both protects against anxiety but allows for the pleasurable release of tension. Freud wrote:

> The Creative writer does the same as the child at play. He creates a world of Phantasy which he takes very seriously – that is, which he invests with large amounts of emotion – while separating it sharply from reality . . . The unreality of the writer's imaginative world, however, has very important consequences for the technique of his art; for many things which, if they were real, could give enjoyment, can do so in the play of Phantasy, and many excitements which, in themselves, are actually distressing, can become sources of pleasure for the hearers and the spectators at the performance of a writer's work.
>
> (Freud, 1908, p. 143)

What makes art different from play or daydreaming is the way in which the artist makes use of the formal organization of the phantasies to soften their impact, and paradoxically to provide an opportunity for enjoyment in the place of anxiety and defense (see recent research by Kounios and Beeman, 2010, regarding the importance of positive affect in the readiness for insight and creative thinking). Freud wrote:

> The writer softens the character of the egoistic daydreams that he offers us in the presentation of his phantasies. We give the name of an incentive bonus, or a fore-pleasure, to a yield of pleasure such as this, which is offered to us as to make possible the release of still greater pleasure arising from deeper psychological sources. In my opinion, all the aesthetic pleasure, which a creative writer affords us, has the character of a fore-pleasure of this kind, and our actual enjoyment of an imaginative work proceeds from a liberation of tensions in our minds. It may even be that not a little of this effect is due to the writer's enabling us thenceforward to enjoy our own daydreams without self-reproach or shame.
>
> (Freud, 1908, p. 152)

In other words Freud viewed art as a variation of the secondary process found in dreams. Unlike dreams, however, creative work involves maintaining awareness of the difference between the real and unreal, while at the same time creating an experience where the difference is partially and temporarily breached. This is the realm of art; the formal organization of the phantasies creates an aesthetic experience, in which the audience can indulge in a conscious and enjoyable experience of dream fulfillment. The piece of literature, the artwork, is simultaneously phantastic and real.

Unfortunately, Freud stops short in his discussion and does not consider the psychological nature of the "arts poetica" which he linked to the overcoming of repressions. The experience of aesthetic pleasure involves not only a release of tension but also the sustained enjoyment of a form of idealization, in which the object is over-valued and esteemed, even while it expresses a range of emotions and phantasies, from the most sublime to the most horrible. Freud never explains this process. Later, I will argue that the primary means by which the artist accomplishes this is through a special idealizing process. He expresses the Phantasy in a form that both expresses the Phantasy but also "makes it special". In this way art creates experience that amalgamates Phantasy and idealization.

With ego psychology, the psychoanalytic emphasis began to shift to art as an activity of the ego (Kris 1952; Sachs 1942). Nonetheless, creativity continued to be linked to the dynamics of the primary process, albeit now altered by defense mechanisms. According to ego psychologists such as Freiberg and Kris, art involves a *regression in the service of the ego* (Kris 1952) in which primitive drive impulses in the form of fantasies are consciously channeled and organized according to the rules of social communication and culture. To them, art is primarily a product of the secondary process acting upon primary-process fantasies.

The work of the ego psychologists, most especially that of Kris, contributed an important facet to the psychoanalytic model of art – that is, that the creation of art involves a dynamic interaction between conscious and unconscious thought processes, between fantasy and reality. This is crucial, given that successful art must "work" according to conditions and terms that are radically different from those of the unconscious or of sleep. Art exists for the real world, and ego psychologists understood this.

At the same time, from the perspective of object relations theory, Melanie Klein (1929, 1930) viewed art as a function of the psychological dynamics of the depressive position. In a model later extended by Hanna Segal (1952, 1957), the Kleinians viewed the search for order and beauty as an attempt to reconstitute and preserve an internal good-object world, threatened with permanent disintegration as a result of the aggressive forces of the paranoid-schizoid position. What is important for us to note in this approach is the notion that creativity and art have a dynamic, integrative function in which the artist works to achieve an enhanced form of self-experience by means of creative activity.

On the other hand, D. W. Winnicott (1971), diverging from the Kleinian viewpoint, proposed a special relationship between the inner world of the artist and the object of his or her creation. For Winnicott, an artwork can be understood as a type of *transitional object*, which is experienced by the artist as a part of the self, an object invested with fantasy. Creativity arises from the fluid relationship between the fantasy life of the artist and the plastic nature of the potential artwork. Creativity occurs in the transitional or potential space between the artist's inner fantasies and the world of objects. This is where the capacity to play is important.

Consistent with classical tradition, for Winnicott, unconscious processes (fantasizing, in this case) influence the artist's relationship with the world, altering the formal structure of reality to express subjective processes. Unfortunately, despite the richness of Winnicott's model, he does not differentiate between the creativity of the artist and the everyday creative engagement of an individual with his or her world. Given this limitation – although Winnicott offers us a stimulating view of human psychology – we remain disappointed by his failure to speak to the special quality found in the creation of art.

In 1980, Gilbert Rose published the first edition of his monograph *The Power of Form* (all quotes will be from the expanded 1992 edition), in which he offered a model of creativity as a distinct psychological process. Rose's work is a transition from the ego psychological and object relations perspectives toward a self-psychological model of the creative process. This is due to the emphasis that Rose places on the role of narcissism in creativity. He wrote:

> Unconscious remnants of the so-called omnipotent feelings of infancy can be seen to play an important role in the impulse to create. Whereas before, they

> were grandiose notions of the person the child thought him- or herself to be, they have become transformed into perfectionist goals to which the child aspires in order to earn self-respect. The artist endows his or her work with this ego ideal of perfection.
>
> (p. 63)

Echoing the Kleinian model, Rose believed that the artist is seeking to recover the experience of early states of perfection in which the child feels at one with an idealized, all-powerful mother. This is not to say that creativity implies psychopathology or developmental deficit. Rather, Rose (1992) believed that:

> Everyman has undergone separation from what was primordial, unitary pre-self, each of us is, so to speak, bereft of our original partner. Our imperfection, then, is our incompleteness, and seeking self-completion is the route (back) to *perfection*.
>
> (p. 67) (emphasis mine)

Unlike Klein, Rose did not think that aggression played a central role in creativity. To him, the loss of perfection formed a part of individuation and the establishment of self-experience.

The artist, according to Rose, is someone who turns inward to experience the early state of fusion, and thus to "gain an increased apprehension of the nature of reality" (p. 69). This is not just a private fantasy, but also an exploration of primitive fusion states of maternal oneness and bisexuality through which the artist "reshapes reality in new forms" (p. 69). Rose stated: "The re-emergence from narcissistic fusion and the re-establishment of ego boundaries carry the possibility of altered, perhaps even innovative, arrangements of the building blocks of reality" (p. 70). He continued:

> By making the work serve as a proxy, the artist can vicariously relive the primitive experiments of testing reality by repeated fusions and separations. The artwork is built up and melted down again and again, repeating second-hand the building up and melting down of psychic structure in the emergence from narcissism . . . In other words, the artist searches for self-completion in the work; he or she has a private dialogue with a projected part of self-mirroring, smiling, frowning, approaching, and withdrawing, until the final completion and release.
>
> (p. 73)

Here Rose described how the artist engages in a dialectical process with the artwork, which is composed of the projected contents of the artist's psyche. In this way, the artist engages in an act of self-creation through structure building, both internal and external. Rose seemed to be describing a dialogue in which the artist creates the object as he creates his self. However, it is not just the artist's own self, but the universal human self-making process that is captured in the artwork.

> The artwork summarizes and magnifies the process by which each of us continually tests and masters reality, relating inner and outer in repeated fusions and separations. The creative work that remains behind represents the cast of a mind "reborn" and objectified in the process of thought, feeling and action.
>
> (pp. 77–78)

From the perspective of Self Psychology, Heinz Kohut argued for the special role of self-experience in the creative process. Kohut felt that the creative person possesses a more fluid self-structure, characterized by dynamically active, archaic modes of psychological organization. He believed that the artist's relationship to the world was narcissistically driven and that the boundaries between self and object were less rigid:

> In creative work narcissistic energies are employed which have been changed into a form to which I referred earlier as idealizing libido. The creative individual is less separated from his surroundings than the non-creative one; the "I-You" barrier is not as clearly defined. The creative individual is keenly aware of these aspects of his surroundings that are of significance to his work and he invests them with narcissistic-idealizing libido.
>
> (1966, p. 112)

At the heart of artistic creativity, Kohut believed, the artist seeks an experience of perfection, or rather the experiencing of a lost, ideal self-state:

> Creative artists may be attached to their work with the intensity of an addiction and they try to control and shape it with forces and for purposes, which belong to the narcissistically experienced world. They are attempting to re-create a perfection that formerly was directly an attribute of their own.
>
> (1985, p. 115)

Kohut envisioned a form of psychological process that characterizes the internal psychological life of the artist. This process involves movement from states of self-cohesion to fragmentation and depletion, to periods during which the self is able to reinvest the work with renewed energy. He elaborated these ideas as follows:

> The psychic organization of some creative people is characterized by a fluidity of the basic narcissistic configurations, i.e., that periods of narcissistic equilibrium (stable self-esteem and securely idealized internal values; steady, persevering work characterized by attention to detail) are followed by

> (precreative) periods of emptiness and restlessness (decathexis of values and low self-esteem; addictive perverse yearnings: no work), and that these, in turn, are followed by creative periods (the unattached narcissistic cathexis which had been withdrawn from the ideals and from the self are now employed in the service of the creative activity: original thought; intense passionate work). A phase of frantic creativity (original thought) is followed by a phase of quiet work (the original ideas of the preceding phase are checked, ordered and put into communicative form, e.g., written down), and that this phase of quiet work is in turn interrupted by a fallow period of precreative narcissistic tension, which ushers in a phase of renewed creativity, and so on.
>
> (1977, p. 815)

At the present time, we understand this process as an unfolding experience of self-cohesion, self–object failure, restoration, and renewed self-experience. Kohut's model of artistic creativity stresses the relationship between self–object failure and restoration.

Charles Kligerman was the first to devote a paper to the development of a self-psychology of art. Essentially in agreement with Kohut, Kligerman (1980) described four characteristics of creativity:

> An intrinsic joy in creating. This is perhaps the most important factor, but the one we know least about.
>
> The exhibitionistic, grandiose ecstasy of being regarded as the acme of beauty and perfection and the nearly insatiable need to repeat and confirm this feeling.
>
> The need to regain a lost paradise – the original bliss of perfection – to overcome the empty feeling of self-depletion and to recover self-esteem. In the metapsychology of the self, this would amount to healing the threatened fragmentation and restoring firm self-cohesion through a merger with the self-object – the work of art – and a bid for mirroring approval of the world.
>
> We can also add a fourth current to the creative drive – the need to regain perfection by merging with the ideals of the powerful selfobjects, first the parents, then later revered models that represent the highest standards of some great artistic tradition.
>
> (1980, pp. 387–388)

Kligerman's chapter opened the way to a new perspective on art, in which the artist actively seeks to bring about an experience to confirm and/or repair his or her sense of self. Rather than a regressive phenomenon, creativity is a complex, high-level psychological activity that attempts to create an experience in which a fragile or precarious self is linked to an ideal object, to idealized relationships, and to ideal values. As a result of the successful creative effort, the artist experiences him- or herself as renewed, confirmed, and revitalized. Kligerman's psychology of the artist is based on a model of developmental psychopathology; however, he suggests that the drive to create may occur without serious self pathology, and that it may be engaged in as an end in itself.

In 1988, Carl Rotenberg sought to develop a more elaborate self-psychological model of creativity. Rather than viewing art from a purely clinical perspective, Rotenberg recognized the "powerful organizing influence that visual arts have for the self" (p. 195). Focusing primarily on the viewer of art, he argued for the important role of creativity and art appreciation in normal human psychology. For example, consistent with Kohut's viewpoint that self-objects play a role not just in an archaic developmental sense, but throughout life – even in the psychological lives of emotionally healthy adults – Rotenberg noted that both the artist and the viewer seek out the confirming, vitalizing, and transformative functions of the aesthetic selfobject experience. He believed that they do so not to cope with pathology, but rather as a healthy, affirmative, and vital experience in and of itself.

In addition, Rotenberg saw the selfobject function of art as embedded in a *shared experiential space* between the subjectivity of the viewer and the artist. The point at which these multiple subjectivities come together, of course, is the experience of the artwork itself. The question is in what sense the artwork contains or reflects the subjectivity of the artist. In this regard, Rotenberg (1988) had something quite interesting to say:

> [The artist] puts his own puzzles and mental ambiguities outside of himself and then reacts to them as of they were other than his. In a sense, once the artist begins a work, he surrenders to it as though the work were dominating him, demanding the solution of its own ambiguities, and requiring completion. The artist experiences the selfobject functioning of the artwork as alive, active, interpretive and eventually having transformational capabilities, to the extent that inner puzzles of the artist are worked out through this externalization. (p. 209)

Thus, Rotenberg had begun to identify the internal dynamics of the creative process, though not in the traditional terms of intrapsychic life; rather, he was talking about the dialectical relationship between the artist and evolving artwork, in which aspects of the artist's subjectivity are externalized as artistic form. Rather than seeing the artist as surrendering to the work, my view is that the artist engages in a process in which internal and externalized aspects of self-experience enter into a dialectical relationship that transforms both. Successful creation is determined by the symbolic articulation of feeling, of the vital experience of living made manifest through the completed artwork.

Psychoanalysis has had important things to say about art, and I believe that any adequate model of art must address the issues that we have discussed. Let me summarize some of the major findings of psychoanalytic aesthetics.

(1) Fundamental to the psychoanalytic view is the notion of the expression of unconscious fantasy in symbolic form – that which was internal (mental) is

externalized. In art, these symbols are expressed in language or other artistic forms that may vary with regards to the explicit or implicit expression of fantasy.

(2) There is a dynamic relationship between the work and the conscious ego, which is enlisted in the service of unconscious fantasy and desire. The primary mechanism for this process is sublimation in which fantasy is transformed into art as a means to express desire in an acceptable form. In other words, art becomes a means by which the person manipulates and manages mental states and fantasies – thus conscious and unconscious thinking is expanded.
(3) The creation of art plays a role in self-repair and self-restoration. The creative process replicates aspects of early experiences of attachment and separation, most importantly, the role that these early interactions play in restoring self-experience in the face of loss, separation and trauma. In other words, art is a means by which the mind and self are maintained, elaborated and repaired when necessary.
(4) The creation and enjoyment of art is a means by which the artist and audience express, elaborate and sustain self-experience.

However, many of these important observations are secondary to art's essential place in human psychological and social life and/or they are not an exclusive or unique function of art. Other non-art experiences perform the same functions. In fact this points to the most important problem in psychoanalytic approaches to art – by failing to identify what makes art unique, most writers essentially select some psychological dimension of art and promote it as a defining attribute.

If we identify a common theme in the four findings of psychoanalysis that I have listed above it would be this: art involves the expression of subjectivity (e.g., fantasies, mental imagery, conscious and unconscious thought) into something external, an object that contains subjective elements (e.g. symbols). Simultaneously the externalized subjectivity (the art work) is manipulated according to a dynamic relationship that it has to the artist's subjective experience. One crucial aspect of this process, which psychoanalysis fails to adequately address, is the artist's perfection of the artwork, and the relationship between the quality of the artwork and the artist's inner life, especially his aesthetic needs and motivations. I believe that it is the element of "perfecting" that distinguishes art from other psychological processes such as dreaming, symptom formation, and other psychological defenses and mechanisms. We will discuss this in more detail later.

There is a remarkable consistency between the psychoanalytic understanding of art and the findings of other sciences. The interested reader will find in the appendix a review of some recent research into the biological and evolutionary sources of art, locate the origin of art in the earliest attachment drives and interactions, describe the unique psychological processes and characteristics of art making, and show how, through art, these attachment states are elaborated and extended to social relations and mature psychological health.

In the following section I will show how despite the fact that art can never replace relationships with others, nor heal real psychological damage, it is nonetheless one of the most important means by which human beings give meaning and value to their lives, not just through some secondary functions, but through the value and power that art possesses as an elementary human striving.

What art is

> What does it mean to express one's idea of some inward or "subjective" process? It means to make an outward image of this inward process for oneself and others to see; that is, to give the subjective events an objective symbol. It is an outward showing of inward nature, an objective presentation of subjective reality. It is the created image that has elements and patterns like the life of feeling. But this image, though it is a created apparition, a pure appearance, is objective; it seems to be charged with feeling because its form expresses the very nature of feeling. Therefore, it is an *objectification* of subjective life.
>
> (Langer, 1957, p. 9)

Art is a psychological process that a person engages in as part of a special type of interaction with the world. During the initial phase of the creative process an artist invests the world with subjectivity – he does this with a particular type of gesture (e.g. a swipe of paint on a canvas, a written phrase, a series of notes, etc.). This new element, the artist's externalized subjectivity, becomes the focus of his creative attention and work. Susanne Langer describes how the artist creates "expressive form, or apparent forms expressive of human feeling". However, this process becomes art only when the internal subjectivity of the artist engages the external subjectivity of the new object in dialectic during which inner and outer subjective elements interact and change each other – gesture follows and builds on the previous gesture, the artwork gradually crystallizing as a network of gestures. The direction of change in the artwork is always toward perfecting, or "making special". As a result, the artist's subjectivity is expressed, elaborated and refined. The artist who engages in such a psychological process does so by making use of certain types of opportunities to create art.

Subjectivity, or "human feeling", is not simply emotion or affect. Langer described it as "the actual felt process of life, the tensions interwoven and shifting from moment to moment, the flowing and slowing, the drive and directedness of desires, and above all the rhythmic continuity of our selfhood" (p. 133).

Human activity always involves some degree and type of projection in which the experience of the object is given organization and meaning. In other words we are not passive recipients; rather we actively construct our experience of reality according to an infinite store of templates and organizing principles based on our past experiences combined with neurological readiness to experience the world in certain ways. Although ultimately we cannot separate these subjective components of experience from the "thing itself", it is possible to emphasize one or the other in our dealings with the world. Thus, the artist is a person who attempts to perfect the articulation of subjectivity in experience.

When we talk about the expression or objectification of subjectivity, what do we mean? In his quote on p. 6, Gilbert Rose argued that self-experience becomes real and sustains itself by means of objective patterns of behavior. In this light I suggest that one way to view subjectivity in art is through the concept of gesture – in particular that artists use a series of related gestures to create any form of art, and that it is the residue of those gestures that composes the artwork.

Gesture is:

(1) a movement or position of the hand, body, head, or face that is expressive of an idea, opinion, emotion, etc.;
(2) the use of such movements to express thought, emotion, etc.; and
(3) any action, courtesy, communication intended for effect or as a formality, considered expression, on demonstration.

I would extend this definition to all forms of subjective expression. In fact there is no way to conceive of the expression of subjectivity except as a gesture of some type. The first and most fundamental forms of gesture are physical, having to do with the body – limbs, face, head movements. It is at the level of bodily interaction that the earliest forms of communication through gesture occur and it remains the substrate (and subtext) of all forms of human gesture. Thus it is through gesture that subjectivity is expressed and made real. For our purposes I believe that the expressive dimension of art is gesture. Once again the most familiar, restrictive form of gesture is bodily action, but I believe that gesture also includes any activity in which the environment is given form through expressive action (the use of words, other symbols, sounds, etc.). Thus it is not the content of an expression that is gesture, but the content as expressed through movement and action. In other words meaning is inseparable from gesture. However, gesture requires a medium. Whether that medium is as basic and personal as a limb, or a tube of fluorescent light, or the evocation of an idea through the display of a found object, in each case subjectivity requires a *means* of expression. The artist makes use of a medium to express subjectivity and this making use of the medium is manifest as *Gesture*. Once this is understood, we can go a step further to say that subjectivity is perfected through the refinement of the expressive qualities of gesture.

Gesture is important to the experience of the self. We come to know ourselves though our perception of our own gestures, most importantly our gestures in relation to other people and their responsive gestures in turn. Our bodies, words and behaviors, ever changing and loaded with emotion and intention, are observed and linked to who we are, and most importantly, to who we are in the minds of others. In other words, gestures are fundamentally implicit, procedural forms of self-experience, and hence we may not be conscious of the meanings of our gestures, given that gestures are linked to emergent and preconscious expressions of self-in-the-world. Most importantly it is gesture in vocalizations, body movement, and facial expressions that is the means by which we communicate self-states, and influence each other's internal representational worlds. D. W. Winnicott (1971) spoke of "the spontaneous gesture" as an action involving a feeling of authenticity. He believed that this authentic response, originating in an untrammeled (as yet uninhibited) part of the self, is the source of creativity and the sensation of being real. The mother's response to the infant's spontaneous gestures facilitates the infant's creativity and sense of selfhood (and prevents the necessity for the development of restrictive, protective self-organization) – this spontaneous gesture, however, is simultaneously simple and unimaginably complex. As Peter Fonagy wrote:

> Babies become sensitive to the distinctive internal patterns of physiological and visceral stimulation that accompany discrete emotion expressions through the application of the contingency-detection mechanism to the contingent relation between automatic emotion expressions of the infant on the one hand, and the caretaker's consequent affect-reflective facial/vocal displays on the other.
>
> (Fonagy *et al.*, 2003, p. 219)

In other words, we come to know ourselves, especially our internal emotional lives, through interactions with others when they respond to our emotional expressions with their own emotional responses. Our sense of self, our internal representational world, crystallizes through this interchange of gestures. In fact, thinking itself is given form through psychological structures or organizations of meaning that have form and gestural qualities. As a result, my thoughts look and feel different from yours. They have their own form and texture, rhythm and tone; in this sense, thoughts also bear the signature of the self. They become a way I know to reflect on my self – and the gestural quality of thought is an important way that I am a self.

It is important to recognize that our earliest gestures occur within the context of intimate caretaking relationships. We act toward and with others, and the response of these others helps to invest our gestures with meaning. We grow concerned with how others are experiencing and judging us. This interactional engagement is composed of gestures which are emergent and which reflect the feelings and thoughts between us. Hungry gestures, loving gestures, angry gestures, sexual gestures, are the meat and drink of our relationships. In other words we live through gesture. We know ourselves, our relationships, and our worlds by means of the gestures out of which our selves crystallize and evolve. Normally we take gestures for granted. Artists make gesture the object of their creative efforts, the refined articulation of gesture becomes the means for the most powerful expression of human meaning. However, although the artist's use of gesture has its roots in these fundamental intersubjective processes we have been describing, what the mature artist brings to his or her work with gesture is far more complex and advanced.

The artist channels these spontaneous gestures within the disciplines, methods, and contexts of his professional training and practice. Through effort and devotion to craft, a repertoire of gestures is constructed and the artist brings to those gestures a practice of recognition and selection built on a lifetime of experience. Once the gesture or impulse has caught his attention, he works on it through a disciplined creative process that only years of study and practice can attain. The deepest sources of gesture are in the spontaneous, physical processes and responses to living; as we mature and grow, we refine our gestures, they come to reflect who we are in body and mind, are molded in the crucible of relationships, and are further refined through knowledge, discipline, practice, criticism and appreciation. For the artist gesture is the vehicle of meaning, fully integrated into craft and elaborated by creative effort. The artist "makes use" of his own gestural repertoire (implicit and explicit). At the same time he allows his body and mind to respond, to react, to make mistakes – to create the readiness for new, as yet unseen, gestures. The artist uses what he knows and what is "at hand", but he also creates the conditions for surprise out of this generative complexity.

When we say that art begins with the externalized subjectivity of the artist we are not just talking about feeling or emotion. The artist's subjectivity is the personal experience of being. It is the sense of self both as body and being-in-the-world. In this sense the artist is just like us: all human actions have a subjective signature, the unique quality that each individual possesses. The artist makes that subjective signature the focus of creative work, and by means of the creative process the artist's being is articulated and refined. In the best of cases, we experience the artwork as an exquisite and powerful aesthetic experience – human being communicated with power and grace.

These complex and mature artistic gestures possess cultural, relational and individual dimensions (metasubjective, intersubjective and intrasubjective dimensions). Yet gestures are usually ambiguous – this may be an asset for the artist, even while he is not sure where the gesture is "going" or what it will ultimately "mean". Gestures can be broad, large and sweeping, or they can be focused, contained and brief. As the artwork develops, gestures accumulate and affect each other, and the crystallizing gestural gestalt may possess qualities quite different from the individual gestures out of which it is composed. All creative gestures are grounded in implicit, procedural knowing, passing under the cognitive radar (so to speak) but then at other times becoming startlingly present and clear. The artist's understanding of his own gestures is complex and evolving. Implicit expression is followed by deliberate conscious expression, conscious assessment and review. New ways of seeing and knowing emerge, additional accidental or spontaneous actions are taken, more reassessments are done and rejected, doubt is followed by fleeting associations, then more gestures, revisions, and then unexpectedly the artist sees something, and says to himself, "What the hell is that? Did I do that?" Then he formulates an idea, an understanding of the work – "Oh, that's what I am trying to say!" – and continues, all the time searching for the best way to say something, to get it right.

Another way of looking at Gesture in art involves the creation of a *subjective object.* It is in the formal aspects of the *subjective object* that the dimensions of subjectivity of the artist are externalized – the artwork is a concretization of many interrelated gestures. This process of externalization through the medium of art inevitably results in accidents and other unanticipated emergent phenomena. In other words gestures are imperfect and lead to unexpected consequences. Once the subjective object is "out there", existing separately from the artist's inner world, it can be acted upon and its form manipulated in order for the artist's internal and now external subjectivity to be perfected and refined. In a practical sense the artist tries to do his best, to produce the best piece of work of which he or she is able. In other words, the artist seeks to perfect the artwork, to make it the best, most ideal it can be. In the same way the infant seeks from mother the reciprocal mutual idealizing experiences, the perfecting of the artwork is a pleasurable and self-affirming activity (a selfobject experience).

Perfection in art involves a complex organization of values that the artist has internalized and integrated into his *artistic self* (the artist's professional self-organization (Roland, 2003)). There is a feedback loop in which the new object influences the artist even as the artist further refines the object – an aesthetic resonance. This responsiveness has its roots in the mother's response to the infant's spontaneous gesture. It also shares characteristics of their expressions of mutual admiration. At least temporarily the artist feels more alive and more cohesive as a person when the creative process goes well. Inevitably the experience of resonance fails, resulting in anxiety and self-crisis, provoking the artist to renew his search for a restored selfobject tie through further refinements of the art work. This dialectic between the artist's subjectivity and his or her externalized subjectivity in the crystallizing work, results in the emergence of new formal elements and unique organizations of experience, until then unknown or unseen even by the artist. These emergent, unexpected elements either resonate with the artist's subjectivity, or cause disruption or renewed creative effort. This entire process results in the perfection of an increasingly ideal object the formal aspects of which embody perfected gestures, enhanced manifestations of human subjectivity. Thus through the arts self-experience is elaborated and refined. As Terrance Deacon noted:

> The arts appear to continually expand the space of emergent emotional states we can experience. This ever-expanding exploration of newly emergent experience is clearly one of art's great attractions. It is literally an exercise in expanding the space of consciousness.
>
> (Deacon, 2006, pp. 50–51)

Nonetheless, the successful artwork is not synonymous with or equivalent to the artist's self. Instead it is entirely new, independent and unique, an ideal product, and – given this – a highly refined and perfected "making real" of human subjectivity itself. The artwork, being the product of the artist, does essentially mirror the artist's creative self (albeit in its complex, ambiguous and protean nature) and even its externality becomes an important benefit to the artist, who can hold to the phantasy that the fragile and ever-changing uncertainty of his or her inner life and sense of self is now permanently contained and embodied in this special, ideal object.

This does not mean that all artists are happier because they make art. However ephemeral the positive emotions may be, I believe that making art does contribute to feelings of well being and this is one of the main reasons that the career of an artist can have such a strong appeal to persons who have attachment disorders and/or traumatic backgrounds. For them, successful art making can provide experiences of psychological wholeness and vitality, as well as a sense of attachment to a special other. In modern times particularly, the highly individualized nature of artwork and creativity has meant that the experience of the artist has become increasingly individualized and idiosyncratic. Through art, the artist externalizes aspects of his or her subjectivity and imagination. It is thus aspects of the self that are refined, perfected and made special. Therefore, for modern artists it is possible to achieve a powerful self-affirming and self-vitalizing experience.

Artists with traumatic or neglectful early attachment relationships may find the activation of biologically based aesthetic organizing principles as a result of making art, and thus a longed-for solution to a lifetime of anxiety, isolation and pain. For these people, artistic work can feel powerfully organizing, emotionally stimulating and self-confirming. In instances when the artist is "talented", the gratification of these longed-for selfobject experiences becomes possible through art.

Despite the highly positive experience that may result from art, it is no replacement for relationships with other people; or for that matter self-structure that is absent or damaged. Successful artistic creativity is a potent but nonetheless temporary and highly transient fix. However, given the intermittent nature of the reinforcement, art making can become compelling, even addictive.

"Making Special" and the psychological role of idealization

As we have seen all creative artists seek to make something special or ideal. At the same time some artists are not satisfied with reproducing earlier art works: they want to produce something unique and fresh, something new. In modern art this was what was most highly prized, especially by certain parts of the newly emergent art world.

Creating something new can be both difficult and stressful. The modern artist, seeking to develop radically different art forms, intentionally rejected many of the conventions and support that artists had traditionally relied on in their work.

The most common guide became self-reflection by means of dialectic between externalized aspects of subjectivity, amalgamated with a medium as part of the emerging artwork, and internal responses, such as reveries, fantasies, or intuitive affective reactions. Modern artists intentionally repudiated the lingering residue of formal education and traditional values, in favor of a spontaneous and even chaotic engagement with the artwork. This revolution in art challenged traditional ideas of aesthetic quality and subverted the very notion of valid criteria for judgments of taste.

Psychoanalysis has not been of much help in this regard. Although it can be useful in interpreting the content of art, especially the unconscious sources of imagery, narrative, and so forth, it tells us almost nothing regarding the criteria for *bad* as opposed to *good* art. And while no theory or model may ever be a reliable evaluative guide, it should at least provide us with a means to discuss the place of artistic quality in the experience and investigation of art. Susanne Langer noted this problem in 1942:

> An analysis to which the artistic merit of a work is irrelevant can hardly be regarded as a promising technique of art-criticism, for it can only look to the hidden content of the work, and not to what every artist knows as the real problem – *the perfection of form*, which makes this form "significant" in the artistic sense.
>
> (Langer, 1942, p. 208)

Normally our awareness and experience of our subjectivity (e.g. self-reflection, or self-consciousness) is a process to which we do not attend directly (much of what we call consciousness goes on unreflectively). However, some practices seek to help us sharpen, control and otherwise manage our consciousness (meditation is one example). Normally we do this through manipulating our self-reflective capabilities and, to some extent, controlling our thoughts and feelings. Artists use art to externalize subjectivity, and as subjectivity becomes objectified, the artist "perfects" aspects of subjectivity that are part of the object. What do I mean in this instance by "perfecting"?

Art is experienced as beautiful when the formal aspects of the art work, that which expresses the artist's perfected subjectivity, approaches or achieves an ideal. Beauty is the perfect result of the creative process. In art, human subjective life – human being – achieves its purest articulation in the experience of beauty.

Many artists find the notion of perfection threatening. Especially in modern western culture, the highly personalized and expressive nature of art leads to a rejection of anything that might confine or control the artist's creativity. The idea of perfection still evokes the competitions and judgments of the academie in nineteenth-century Europe, which prompted the rebellion of the impressionists and post impressionists. However, in most cultures, the artist is a special person skilled in creating certain types of perfected objects or experiences. In fact

Dissanayake (2000, 2009) argued that "making special" (e.g. perfecting, refining, idealizing) something is the defining feature of art (see the appendix for an extended discussion of Dissanayake's work).

On a practical, work-a-day level the artist's search for perfection is simply the desire to do the best job possible. It is impossible to conceive of an artist who does not seek to create the best work he can. However, a modern artist does not judge the success of his artwork according to some prescribed standard of perfection but according to its own individual quality – that is the extent to which he has been successful in creating a work that embodies the best of his own artistic abilities. Over-investment in some notion of perfection can inhibit the artist and avoidance of risk can block innovation. Hence the real (imperfect) and the ideal (perfect) are always in a state of tension. Paradoxically, imperfection in an artwork may accentuate its perfection.

Artists work within a culture. The particular culture provides not just the resources, supplies and means of creating art, but also the values, traditions and aesthetic standards that have been developed and promulgated over time. All artists are both constrained and challenged by these cultural realities. Even the most innovative art is referenced to the cultural context.

Of course the influences on the individual artist are variable and complex. Although he or she will hold to artistic standards derived from biology, culture and relationships, these standards are filtered through a flexible response to the creative process and the encounter with the developing artwork. In addition, the artist has a dynamic relationship to his body, culture and relationships that will also lead to a variable commitment to the standards that he holds.

In summary, the artist's process of refinement or perfection of any particular artwork is highly complex. In modern times artists have been quite radical in subverting all forms of artistic and aesthetic standards and values. Of course this is not true for every artist over time and across cultures: some artists, such as practitioners of the Japanese tea ceremony, emphasis the perfection that comes from total commitment to a culturally based art form where the signs of individual subjectivity are almost completely eliminated. So when we say that an artist seeks perfection in their artwork, we mean something highly variable and multi-determined.

All artists work with a rich source of subjective materials (values, fantasies, affects, memories, sensations, etc.) that will impact on the outcome of the creative process. The artist's context and the balance between the several dimensions of subjectivity that we have discussed influence the determination of the quality of any artwork. If we look at art across history and culture we would see that art always involves a process of perfection but the nature of that perfection is ever changing and elusive. In some instances the standards that determine the quality of art in one generation will be repudiated in the next, in others, standards and notions of art will remain fixed and endure over many generations. Both situations are true of art.

This is not to say that in art "anything goes". Human beings can only create meaning within a context and most importantly within a culture and among other people. Meaning depends on some accepted types of symbols and rituals – as well as standards of quality in their expression. Even the most radical modern artist is bound by the social world in which he lives. At the very least any revolution will have to occur in reference to some social standards that will partially define the nature of the rebellion (would Duchamp's urinal mean anything without the aesthetic standards he was highlighting and undermining?). The bottom line may be that even in the most anarchistic cultures art will be held to some biologically based standards of perception and feeling which will influence how an artist and his audience evaluate the quality of art. This would explain how across history and culture the best forms of art appeal to most people. We can experience art from foreign societies yet feel its beauty. Again, these qualities are enormously varied and complex, but they seem to reflect some basic artistic values, which always play a part where art is involved.

Conclusion

Art feels good – both for the artist and the audience. It is safe to say that for all artists, the experience of creating art has a far more positive tone than say, having a fine meal. I argue that creativity involves the gratification of psychological needs on many levels. Most importantly, art is a special means of bringing about and experiencing, as an adult, archaic modes of relatedness and self-experience of a powerfully affirming nature.

As discussed, the artistic creative process involves the perfection of objectified subjectivity. If successful, the artist experiences a resonance with his artwork to the extent that his inner self-experience and outer self-reflection mirror each other. In addition, given that the goal of creation is the gradual construction of an ideal artwork, the mirroring that results is of an archaic nature. The wonderful mirror reflects the image of a grandiose self. It is a selfobject experience, as a result of which the artist feels recognized, validated, vitalized and perhaps even loved.

However, successful artistic creativity and the selfobject experience of the artist do not always match. This is because the selfobject experience crystallizes due not to the inherent nature of the artwork but rather to how the artist experiences the creative process and the artwork. Many artists are not good judges of their own work: hence they can experience selfobject failure even when the work they are doing is technically quite good. That said, even where the artist's experience of the artwork and its artistic quality are out of sync, the drive for perfection moves the artist's creative process forward. Where the artist experiences success, the result is a selfobject experience, with the resulting positive psychological self-state.

Chapter 2

Psychoanalysis as creative art

In this chapter I explore how psychoanalysis and psychoanalytic psychotherapy are forms of art, consistent with the definition of art discussed in the last chapter. Most importantly psychoanalysis, like the fine arts, involves the objectification, transformation, and enhancement of subjectivity. This process, as we have seen, is at the heart of the arts – in fact it defines Art as a human activity. In Chapter 7 we will engage in an explicit comparison of artistic processes and analytic processes. Here we will begin with a more general examination.

Over the years many have used Art as a metaphor for analysis and others have discussed the artful qualities of psychoanalytic practice and technique. Certainly it has always been acknowledged that there is an art to psychoanalysis – at least in the general sense of a skillfulness informed by intuition and feeling. But I want to go beyond this approach. I believe that psychoanalysis is an actual art form and that its dynamics – and most importantly its outcomes – are essentially the same as any art form, such as painting, choreography, musical composition, etc. I recognize that many will find this idea strange and perhaps confusing. That is why I have preceded this chapter with a definition of art which explains the commonalities between all of the Arts, including psychoanalysis as we shall see. This definition is a psychological one. I will show that behind the behaviors and products which we associate with the art of analysis there is, in their creation, a set of psychological processes and needs which every artistically motivated person engages in and seeks to satisfy.

Throughout human history all societies have established ways to help their people alleviate emotional distress and cope with problems in their lives. Most prominently religion, associated institutions and rituals have been a powerful means by which people have managed fear, coped with suffering, and sought meaning and value in a world which is filled with disruption, pain, loss and death. Social institutions and specialized groups have also been important. Commonly these are organized according to a particular hierarchy within the community where certain individuals or small group are granted special status, even powers, which have sustained and guided communities. These institutions, rituals and beliefs have sustained people and communities from the beginning of human life on earth. However, up until the present age these resources have focused on the person as an embedded and inseparable part of a community and a culture. For example, the power of faith comes from the way the individual gets strength from the beliefs of the community and the institutional structures, relationships and ritual which supports individual life within the supportive context of the society. However, in the centuries after the Renaissance the nature of individual experience and the sense of selfhood began to change fundamentally. In addition the cultural institutions and beliefs which had been at the center of social and individual life also began to diversify and the cultural resources which had been the solace and refuge for individuals were no longer as meaningful or powerful. Individual subjectivity and the experience of being an independent source of impression, feeling, thought and action became the nature of modern human life.

That being said, individual human beings are generally unable to reflect effectively on their own thoughts and feelings. Although the enlightenment valorized the power of mind it also made clear that perception and the mind are highly unreliable. Hence methods were developed to structure and control perception, and organized thought processes, so that a reliable knowledge of the world could be arrived at. However, methods to reflect accurately and reliably on subjective life were not developed. Individual subjectivity had no means of managing itself. Descartes' method when applied to one's own inner experience is useless: the instrument of observation, being the same thing as the suffering self quickly succumbed to the fog of neurotic conflict.

In the past, when a person began to experience anxiety, depression and hopelessness they would turn to the church. With the decline in religious authority and the increased marginalization of faith in society, there was a need for something new to offer the individual, a way to address problems thrown up by living, inner suffering and troubled relationships. But more importantly what was required was a method for people to deal with problems with this new Self. At the beginning of the twentieth century, psychoanalysis developed to provide just such non-religious support for psychological and emotional suffering. This was the first time in human history that individual subjectivity, at the moment of emergence, in the instant of vital experiencing, was made objective, and thus inner human life could be observed, reflected on and changed. No longer were people left alone to struggle with the ultimately impossible task of self-knowledge. The method Freud invented encouraged the expression of subjectivity, elaborated the subjective in words and actions, organized subjectivity into a meaningful structure through dialogue and interpretation, and then offered a technique to refine these subjective objects – the transferences – work on them, and help the patient do his or her best to get it right, i.e. be less conflicted, feel more self-coherent and alive, and engage with the world more creatively.

Unfortunately human beings are prone to adopt non-creative solutions to life's problems. This is especially true when seeking safety, emotional or otherwise.

Most mental disturbances involve some constriction of the ability to respond creatively to inner states and/or relationships. The primary reason for the collapse of creativity is the desire for security and self-protection. A particular way of thinking or feeling is developed, maintained and even defended as a way to insure that one is psychically and physically safe. If these efforts are successful patients do not come to analysis. For every analysand entering treatment there is some recognition that the strategies he or she has relied on are not working. The defenses which one is clinging to no longer feel acceptable; but for many reasons, the patient cannot change. He or she feels locked into a rigid and unsatisfactory pattern of thinking, feeling and/or acting. The patient may not even be aware of what they are doing, let alone why. But they invariably feel trapped, unable to respond creatively to life's challenges.

Analytic patients do not just show up in our offices without expectation or desire. They come to us hoping for something special: a relationship which will help them to be happier, more effective, feel more confident and sure of their own self-experience, have better sex or be more successful at work. The bottom line is that all patients want to be closer to what they consider "good" – whatever that might be (Hagman, 2000).

In other words, people come to analysts seeking to improve themselves and their lives. They hope that by means of the analytic process they will be freed of the non-creative patterns of feeling and behaving which constrain and torture them. The fantasy is that the analyst and the analytic process possess some power to change their feelings, thoughts and emotions in some decisive sense, which will lead to less pain, more satisfaction and even happiness.

Prior to calling an analyst for an appointment, analysands go through a process of readiness and preparation. In most cases years have passed during which the problem has developed. Sometimes successfully, often not, the analysand has attempted various strategies to feel better or act differently. Ultimately they have proven unsuccessful at least enough to warrant seeking professional help. The call and visit to the analyst must be seen as part of this extended process. In this sense there is a certain readiness as the analysand enters the room. Readiness wrapped in anxiety and self-protectiveness. The analysand is taking action, looking for help, and hoping for change – perhaps without any clear idea about what is going to happen, how change is going to come about, or what that change might be.

That being said, change always involves being "better", feeling happier, being more effective, living life more fully, having better friends, lovers and family relationships. It involves change in the direction of positive self-experience. "I want to feel better about myself and my life" is always at the center of what people want out of analysis. Nonetheless, patients often hide their expectations from us. They have been in many situations in their lives, with people who were supposed to help them be closer to the "good" and they have been disappointed, sometimes hurt, perhaps traumatically so. Yet they walk though our doors, sit down with us and begin talking.

An assumption behind creative analysis is that the very act of showing up is a powerful indication of some desire (however hidden or denied) to be better, do better, and feel better. Although some of these improvements may involve concrete changes in life (a new job, a more loving partner, improved health) it is fundamentally in the subjective realm that patients desire change. They want to experience themselves as happier, more confident, less confused, more assertive, less afraid, etc. It is the ambiguous, conflicted and fractured experience of Self that is their primary concern; they hope that we can help them "get that Self right".

All analysands begin by showing up and telling a story. They enter the analyst's realm, the consulting room, which is where the analyst practices his or her craft. At this point, in this place, the analysand's subjectivity enters into relation with the professional and personal reality of the analyst. The primary tools the analysand uses to express themself is physical and verbal interaction with the analyst. They externalize their inner emotional state so that the analyst can see, and hopefully understand who they are and how they are feeling.

It is also important to note that patients come to analysts because they have been unable to make the desired changes on their own. They may not even know what they want let alone how they can get it. They just know they feel bad about themselves and their lives. What they are hoping for is that the analyst will fix them.

Creative analysis identifies psychological and relational obstacles to creative living and helps to resolve these obstacles, providing a context in which subjectivity can be manifest, elaborated and improved. Ultimately, a successful analysis results in a capacity within the patient to engage in creative living with relative independence. However independence is not really the issue. Creative living is both an individual process and a social process. A creative person can create on his or her own, or be able to engage with others in shared creative efforts.

Another way to think about it is that patients suffer from disorders of creativity. They invariably feel stuck, imprisoned, paralyzed, caught in a repetitive way of thinking, feeling or relating which they know they don't want, but can't come up with an alternative. They are "failed artists of their lives" as Adam Phillips noted. In other words, analytic patients are like artists who suffer from massive, perhaps grotesque, blocks in creativity. They long to live creatively, to respond to life in a way that leads to new experiences and more positive self-states – pride, ambition, joy, excitement – but they find themselves caught in the same old patterns and choices which they feel compelled to make. Creativity is in short supply. They are looking for us to cure these creative disorders.

The analyst is an expert in helping people achieve these types of goals. The primary function of the analytic process is to set the conditions for renewed creative living. As we will see, the analytic method and process is well equipped, and specifically oriented, to safely disrupt non-creative patterns and meanings, manage the ensuing crisis, and eventually reestablish not just a new set of beliefs and behaviors, but an attitude toward self, other and the world which allows for a more flexible, spontaneous and creative life. The renewal of creativity from psychoanalysis is psychologically invigorating; self-experience becomes more cohesive, energized and resourceful.

If we think back to Chapter 1, we can see that psychoanalysis is indeed an art rather than a clinical treatment or a scientific project. It is a process which encourages the expression and externalization of subjectivity, through dialogue and meaning making, so that the subjective experience of the patient can be articulated through the medium of psychoanalysis. In particular, the transference–countertransference relationship is such a subjective/objective "object". It is a rich, complex, ever-evolving structure which drives the analytic process but also becomes the object of attention, reflection and the realm of analytic interaction, and hopefully change. The goal of the process is not just any change, but the improvement of the subjectivity of the patient, the creation of new ways of feeling, thinking and acting which the patient experiences as better than the past. Through the creative process of analysis the subjectivity of the patient is articulated, changed, improved and perhaps even perfected. This is the essence of art. This is what psychoanalytic art is.

In the fine arts, the artist externalizes aspects of his or her subjectivity: a brush stroke, the strike of a chisel, a note on the page. In art, the externalization of the artist's subjectivity as embodied in the artwork is fundamental. The equivalent in psychoanalysis is the mutual offer between the analysand and the analyst of a relationship in which aspects of the analysand's subjective world are shared and elaborated through interaction with the analyst who enters into a relationship with the patient. By means of this intersubjective process the once private experience of the patient becomes externalized within the shared intersubjective field. Over time, as a result of innumerable relational exchanges, the analysand's subjectivity is elaborated as a subjective object, a third self-organization, within the dyadic field. This becomes the object of creative attention and effort. This third, the transference–countertransference relationship, is organized according to both subjectivities in dynamic interaction and reflects the subjectivities of both people. However the function of the analytic process is the elaboration, refinement and development of the analysand with the creative work on this third as the active agent of change.

In other words, different from most forms of art, the creative process in analysis involves two subjectivities in a dynamic relation to a "third" externalized subjectivity that is new and unique to the analytic relationship, emerging from the collaboration of these individual creative agents (Ogden, 1994; Benjamen, 2004). However it is the analyst's job to decenter, using his or her own subjective reactions to understand and make sense of the analysand's subjective world – manifest in the transferential dimension ot this "third" (see Chapter 3 where the capacity to "step away" from experience and think about it is discussed). Empathic immersion, elaboration of an understanding of the analysand's subjective state and process, and responsibility for a meaningful and useful construction of a shared recognition of the analysand's subjectivity is the analyst's role. The patient expresses his or her subjectivity primarily through words and actions. But rather than this expression being directed at an object, or medium, the patient's subjectivity is externalized through its impact on another person, the analyst. The patient speaks, directs a comment or gesture toward the analyst who is thus changed, perturbed, excited, curious, enraged. The patient's subjectivity is now intertwined with the analyst's subjectivity. It is the analyst's job to tease them apart.

The analyst's attitude of neutrality and relative anonymity allows for the patient's subjectivity to be highlighted and made clearer. The analyst accepts the patient's subjectivity and begins to get to know them. Gradually the patient's subjectivity is articulated, given a fuller meaning and put in context in collaboration with the analyst. Over time the analyst comes to "hold in mind" an understanding of the patient's internal world and self-experience. The analyst also actively seeks to draw out and clarify the analysand's subjectivity. In particular, interpretations help to give words to the patient's experience and organize his or her meanings, fantasies and intensions. The analyst's interpretations give the patient an opportunity to reflect on his or her subjectivity, now somewhat changed by the analyst.

In this way the balance of subjectivity in the psychoanalytic dialogue is tipped toward the patient. The process of the dialogue emphasizes the patient's subjectivity far more than the analyst's. The analyst's subjectivity is important, even essential, but its use is primarily as a means to respond, give meaning and assist in the elaboration of the subjective/objective aspect of the treatment. Therefore, the goal of the dialogue is the articulation, understanding and elaboration of the patient's experience and the nature of their subjective life. The analyst is the tool that facilitates this process. It is the analyst's ability to mentalize, to reflect, think about and give words to what may be only a partially conscious experience. This formulates an understanding, an interpretation that is offered back to the patient, who optimally transmutes words into affects and links them to procedural, implicit levels of cognition and fantasy.

This does not mean that the analyst is just a blank screen, far from it. For the patient's subjectivity to be usefully reintroduced to him or her it must also reflect aspects of the analyst's subjectivity which adds credibility and value to the interpretations. In this regard, the patient's most important fantasy is the idea that the analyst possesses a special power to understand and influence. This is the non-specific "positive" transference which is both the binding element in treatment and the facilitator of the analysand's drive to heal and change. It is this dimension of the transference that invests the analyst's interventions with authority and positive value. By means of interpretation the analyst offers back to the analysand a meaningful construction regarding what the analyst has come to believe about the analysand's psychological life. Optimally the analysand experiences the interpretation as both a construction of the analyst as well as an objectified aspect of his or her subjectivity. If the interpretation is authentic and well articulated, and if the analyst captures and communicates accurately the analysand's subjective experience in a manner which the analysand is willing and able to hear, the sense of resonance is amplified, and the interpretation has clout. This type of interpretation is experienced by both analyst and analysand as transcendent, not in a spiritual sense, but in the way that it heightens the degree of value and the intensity of meaning in the relationship and in the analysand's self-experience. It possesses a perfect weight, rightness of meaning, and emotional power. The analysand is "moved" by the interpretation.

Another important aspect of the psychoanalytic art is the active, creative involvement of the patient. Despite the fact that patients suffer from creative disorders and have been stuck for a long time in a rigid and restrictive world, they continue to try to change, albeit without much success. Nonetheless, in treatment, the patient is an active participant in the dialogue. Unless the patient experiences an increased capacity and motivation to engage more creatively in life, the outcome of analysis won't much matter. In fact it is the patient's desire and drive to find solutions and to change, which compels the analyst to react and respond. The dialectic is driven by the analyst's response to the patient's activity, and the way this interaction resonates and amplifies the process. Ultimately, change is made by the patient. It is the patient's desire for improvement, to make things better, to make his or her sense of self more special that is at the heart of the change process. We will discuss the role of the analysand as active change agent and co-creator in Chapter 5.

Case illustration

When Roger entered analysis he was 32 years old. A young entrepreneur, he was the CEO of a "start-up" computer/internet company. Bright and resourceful in his work he had high ambitions. However he was anxious about the practical aspects of his work. Managing staff, dealing with clients and solving mundane problems had made him feel more and more distant from his dream of creating something special, a mirage-like image of a unique product which would embody a longed-for perfection.

I was impressed with Roger's intelligence and drive. He seemed insightful and self-aware. He spoke in sessions with an intensity and sense of purpose. However I began to feel that any comment or interpretation of mine was always "off the mark". In fact he was quick to point out how I had not understood, or that he meant something else. And I would see that he was right. His ability to articulate subtle aspects of meaning in his narrative, that he may not have been clear about, or that I just did not understand, was impressive. I realized repeatedly how right he was, and how wrong I had been.

Of course this made me feel even more tentative and "gun shy". I could not believe that I was so dense and inarticulate. This was surprising to me given that I had been so empathic and "on the mark" with Jim, the patient before Roger in my schedule. How could I go from being so relaxed and insightful, to being such an awkward and dense incompetent?

What we were constructing was a manifestation of Roger's self-state and self-in-relation. He was self-sufficient and felt he was the only one who could solve his problem. By dominating the sessions (not aggressively, but through intelligence and articulateness) he could remain apart from me and not have to engage with another person or, most importantly, depend on them.

Roger grew up in a household dominated by the emotional needs of his mother who suffered from persistent depression and chronic rage which she frequently directed at her son. She would repeatedly point out what she considered to be his flaws and weakness, holding up his older sister as an example to be copied. Roger saw the relationship between his mother and sister as a type of "club" which he was not allowed to join, the membership requirements being impossible levels of compliance and submission to his mother's needs. Over time, he developed a crippling sense of self-doubt and shame at his inadequacies and unworthiness. He recalled many nights when, banished early to his bed, he lay awake hoping for a healing visit from the person who had abandoned him. This state of being, isolated and longing for a visit that never came, began to define Roger's being, his relationship between self and world. The only effective resolution was to encapsulate himself; to manage his painful inner state by denying any need for connection. He was bright and vigilant, and he learned to manage his mother's moodiness and outbursts, steeling himself and suppressing any need to be comforted or cared for. As an adult he was self-critical and apprehensive. He became skillful at observing others' reactions and managing situations to prevent the feared criticism or blame. His intimate relations were with "wounded" women whom he supported and cared for. He never exposed himself, yet he reported to me a persistent sense of loneliness, combined with a fear of rejection by the very women he knew would be best for him. He admitted that he never gave anyone a chance – ultimately this included me.

This transference–countertransference duplicated the familiar, repetitive form of relationships that Roger had been engaged in for many years. It also asserted a familiar and secure self-experience in which he could be self-reliant even while engaging in an ersatz therapeutic relationship with me. My feeling of helplessness and ineffectuality mirrored Roger's own, yet I felt the disturbance since I lacked the skill or access to his inner life that he was unwilling to admit to or share.

This is a good example of the way subjective experience is externalized, manifest in the interaction and organized according to certain beliefs and behavioral patterns. In this sense Roger crafted the psychological organization of the relationship according to templates and models which worked for him – they protected him from vulnerability while affecting some control over his relational world. Just sitting together in the office, week after week, the relationship became a subjective object, a psychological construction which took on a certain consistency and familiarity over time. An important quality of the transference was how non-creative it was and how it confined and limited Roger's experience and self-potential. It "worked" for him but acted in the same way as a warning beacon rotating endlessly in the night serves to protect by calling attention to the invariable threat, it reminded him constantly of the need for vigilance. Often, with people like Roger, the analyst has to wait him out, clarifying the structure and function of the transference, but remaining alert to any disruption or perturbation – usually caused by the emergence of the need for connection and dependence, evoked by the treatment relationship. The experience of disruption, accompanied by long-sequestered longings, provides an opportunity to introduce something new, an interpretation, that might stimulate meaningful change in the direction of positive strivings.

In one session Roger was talking about how isolated he felt. He talked about how much time he spent alone (except for his dog) and how he longed for contact, but always felt unable to trust people. He said the only person he had regular contact with was me, and he stated: "Here I am coming to look for help, and I can't even trust you, George."

I was surprised by his use of my name. I realized that he had never used it before.

"You know Roger, I think that is the first time you have used my name here."

Suddenly something new entered the potential space between us. It was, of course, his intention to use my name, but it had never been uttered between us. It was both a new word, but one associated with me, which indicated that I was on his mind. He acknowledged me and handed me a tool, a new sound or word, which could change everything. I existed as another person who might or might not be "trusted" – implying the possibility of an emotional need for something from me. In another setting, with another type of person, this use of my name may have been unacknowledged, passed unchallenged and unreflected upon. Instead it because an opportunity for creativity.

Once we began to include me in the equation – not as an injured needy lover – but a persistent, interested therapist – all bets were off. I suggested that a person like me had not been part of Roger's life-world, until now. The notion that he would engage me in a joint effort to understand his own experience, not to shame or punish, but to reflect and understand respectfully, threatened to shatter the secure world of splendid isolation which he had cultivated and become skillful at maintaining and managing. He was very anxious about me. He doubted my intentions and worried that even after trusting me, I would fail him, or worse, betray him.

Roger's treatment is an example of analysis as an art form. Over the course of the first months of our work together an objectification of Roger's subjective life, his self-experience, was enacted between us. His private inner struggle and resolution, was made real. It happened in the role, just as if a painting or piece of music had been constructed. It was tangible, had dimensions, form and texture. We came to know the transference, as one would a novel. However, initially it was not creative; it was a construction whose function was not the elaboration and articulation of self-experience, but the entrenched and labored fortification of chronic self-protective measures. This repetitive dimension of transference was meant to resist change, to distance Roger from intimacy, to prevent vulnerability, and control the external world. If Roger had been a writer, seeking advice on a piece of fiction, I would say that he was suffering from lack of vision, imagination and expressive feeling. Worse than writer's block, Roger was stuck rewriting and replaying the same endless scenario, a solipsistic, self-referential tale of ineffectual self-aggrandizement and isolation – with the only audience being himself, a bored frustrated participant in a play gone badly wrong, who longs to go home, but can't find the exit.

What makes analysis so powerful is the introduction of a new person into the plot. This person, the analyst, exists outside the imagination of the analysand, and the omnipotent control of the analysand's fantasy life. He or she is thus in a position to introduce "not-me elements" (Winnicott, 1971) into the analysand's experience. The analyst has been auditioned and assigned a role by the analysand. However they are a different type of character whose role is to enter into the rhythms of the piece, and disrupt the familiar structure of the analysand's self-construction. Over time Roger began to feel a need for me, he permitted the emergence of early longings which he had suppressed for decades. And once these needs were experienced, and importantly allowed to be sustained, in the presence of this new person, me, a process began to unfold which provoked a desire to find a new way, a form of self-experience which included an "other", and which also permitted the arousal of attachment needs which had always been hidden out of fear and the need for vigilance against renewed trauma. From this point Roger no longer experienced self-resonance with the transference. He entered a sustained state of crisis, which it was my job to help manage, containing anxiety and continuing to offer ways to make sense of, and perhaps transform, self-experience and relatedness.

Over time Roger allowed fantasies of connection and longings for trust to enter into our relationship. He struggled to integrate and organize new meanings regarding himself within a close relationship. Psychologically he moved back and forth between rigid self-protection and eagerness to connect and trust. He introduced new transference configurations, new compromises between old organizations of self-experience and new, untested, potential selves. His emotional life became richer and more complex. He experienced an increased sense of pleasure in his daily life and eventually risked entering into a relationship with a woman who proved "right" for him. From the point of view of art, Roger was allowing himself to be more inspired, flexible, and self-critical (in a constructive sense). Each week in session we would elaborate and explore these new self-configurations and my role in them. The scenario of the isolated man walled off from the world evolved as that man struggled with the feelings which other people stirred within him. He was no longer alone but doubts about others' intentions and his need to manage relationships continued. However, gradually he began to articulate a more complex and satisfying way of being, allowing himself to reflect on these changes without rushing to conclusions which served to limit and restrict reality. He became a more successful "artist of his life" as he engaged in more vital, thoughtful and creative relationships and activities.

Conclusion

Many types of art do not produce objects. Music and dance, our most important art forms, are just sound and motion. They are experiences which posess structure and aesthetic quality. In analysis the product is the patient's changing subjective experience, most importantly his or her sense of self. As a result of analysis the self has a structure and even an aesthetic quality quite different from before. The product is not a thing, but a structure of experience. It is the creation, or evocation, of a potential space: a psychological realm within which life unfolds. More specifically, it is a domain of specially prepared subjectivity, which the analyst and patients co-construct and live within. The potential space is a realm in which the old non-creative structures do not fit and therefore do not work very well for the analysand. The transference, rather than being a reliable old method of being, is out of place, awkward and repeatedly subjected to unfamiliar examination and discussion. This space is the between area in a dialectic. It is where the thesis and antithesis meet and interact and within which a new self-structure is formed.

I am not suggesting that the products of analysis should be viewed like paintings or ballets – these phenomena require cultural contexts with special attributes which define them as a type of art work. The Self exists in a different realm and is sanctioned both as the cultural object *par excellence*, but also as an exceedingly private form of experience. That being said, in our time personality has often been included as an art object, the articulation and perfection of the self can have intense cultural value and can even be seen as a commodity in the marketplace alongside other art objects (e.g. Marcel Duchamp felt that being itself was his art). The analytic self is a product of more limited attention and relevance, but it also can be said to possess many qualities that we have come to associate with art work.

1. It is articulated and elaborated within a culturally defined process with methods which possess both effectiveness and quality.
2. The analysand is encouraged to engage with the analyst in co-constructing a sustained, complex structure which is made real within the relationship.
3. This transference is a subjective object, the analysand's self-experience now external to their private subjective life.
4. The analytic self becomes the primary focus of the clinical work.
5. The purpose of analysis is to elaborate and impact on the analysand's self. The analysand's self-experience is changed by the process.
6. This change is both of content but more importantly, quality. The analysand must, in the process, experience themselves as "getting better".
7. The analytic process entails multiple dialectics in this process. Interior/exterior, subjective/objective, self/other, patient/therapist, etc.

8. This ongoing tension and the work of resolution, which it involves, drive the creative process of analysis.
9. The goal of analysis is tied to the sense of "getting it right". The analysand feel sufficiently whole, alive, self-satisfied, effective and well adapted. In other words, a state of having perfected the self reaches a satisfying point, a sense of rightness and fittedness.

Chapter 3

Creative brain

As in art psychoanalytic creativity involves several types of dialectic processes. That between the analysand and analyst, between what is real and what is fantasy, between the subjective and objective dimensions of experience, as well as others not directly discussed (e.g. between past and present, self and other, etc). This chapter reviews recent developments in brain research. As we will see, the nature of brain hemisphere asymmetry and the dynamic interaction of the fundamentally different attitudes of each hemisphere is the physical embodiment of the creative process. In other words, the potential for creativity is hard-wired into brain structure and function. In particular, I will be contrasting Alan Schore's emphasis on the primary role of the right brain in psychotherapy with Iain McGilchrist's argument that creative psychological change always involves left hemisphere and right hemisphere participation. Although a correction of the long-standing tendency to privilege left hemisphere functions (the rational/verbal brain over the relational/emotional brain) is understandable, we will see that it reduces the creative potential of brain function by ignoring the important role of hemisphere differences and interactions in psychological life and clinical processes. Countering Schore's thesis, I will introduce a model developed by Iain McGilchrist which stresses the reverberate relations between the asymmetrical hemispheres, an interaction which is at the heart of creativity. Like Schore, McGilchrist views the right hemisphere as the seat of the self and human relatedness, but it is the left hemisphere which is the problem solver, the part of the brain which disrupts, takes charge and introduces new elements into right hemisphere processes provoking change. In fact, as I will argue, our brains are specifically configured to negotiate living in a complex world. The right brain is at home in ambiguity and affect, the left brain is oriented to make choices, take control and prevail. The two hemispheres, acting in concert, permit us both to attempt to swim in the flow of life and to control our fate. According to McGilchrist the right hemisphere makes us human, but the left hemisphere is a crucial part of the creative process, and the unfolding of human potential. He noted: "everything human involves both hemispheres: we do virtually nothing with one hemisphere alone" (McGilchrist, 2009, p. 210). To place our argument within the context of recent psychoanalytic research into the clinical implications of neuroanatomy I will begin with a review of Schore's work on the role of the right hemisphere in the psychoanalytic process.

Over the past 15 years Allan Schore's several books, numerous articles, and many talks have had an important impact on the world of psychoanalysis and analytic psychotherapy (Schore, 1994, 2003a, 2003b, 2012). Schore explained how neuropsychiatric research has proved that the right and left hemispheres of the brain have not just different functions, but entirely different attitudes and orientations toward reality. The left hemisphere views the world through reason, and is preoccupied with finding the predictable and known, fitting experience into established schemas and making sense of it through language and other symbolic systems. Consciousness finds its home largely in the left hemisphere, though it is a form of consciousness that is dependent on abstractions and has a tenuous tie to reality. Nonetheless, the left hemisphere works hard to figure it all out and put it into words. By contrast, the right hemisphere is the seat of emotional life, self-experience, and social awareness, most notably empathy. Right-hemisphere functioning is largely unconscious (in fact Schore equates the right hemisphere with the Freudian unconscious), but much of the thinking and feeling that allows us to deal with the complexity of relationships and self-feeling originates in the right. A fact that is of crucial importance to Schore's approach is the early maturation of the major functions of the right hemisphere. This development is dependent on interpersonal interactions and the experience of intersubjectivity between child and mother. Research has shown that parental neglect, serious malattunement to affect states, and trauma can impact the phase-appropriate maturation of the capacity for affect regulation and an in-ability to manage states of hyper- or hypoarousal. These vulnerabilities lead to serious problems with self and other regulation, as well as with the ability to relate words to feelings, and to decenter from self in order to empathize with others. In adulthood, people who have experienced a failure in right hemisphere development will struggle to manage moods and affects and to engage in intimate relationships, and will, because of an overreliance on dissociation as a defense, be unable to maintain a positive and stable self-experience. Schore argues that many character-disordered patients suffer from right-hemisphere dysfunctions and that no amount of "talking cure" is going to help them.

Although Schore hints at the relevance of his model for psychotherapy in general, most of his discussion of treatment focuses on patients with severe personality disorders and conditions related to early attachment traumas and failures. For these patients, the experience of trauma during the first years of life, when the right brain is developing at a much more rapid pace relative to the left brain, results in deficits in right-hemisphere structuralization that lead to enduring vulnerability to affect dysregulation, self-disorders, and a crippling reliance on dissociation as a means to manage stress and reduce the disruptions of uncontrollable hyper- or hypoarousal. In light of this, Schore argues that analytic therapists must deemphasize verbal interpretations and focus on affect management, empathic immersion, and assisting the patient with affect regulation and the gradual establishment of new psychological capabilities. He asserts that psychotherapy is a form of right-hemisphere–to–right-hemisphere communication. Through right-hemisphere nonverbal, psycho-biological attunement and "affect synchronizing transactions" the analyst creates the conditions for attachment and eventually for achieving the "long-term goal of reorganizing internal working models into secure models that allow for more complex modes of intrapsychic organizations and interpersonal behaviors, and a developmental progression of the ability, in a variety of familiar and novel contexts, to maintain a coherent, continuous and unified sense of self, a function of the right hemisphere, the biological substrate of the human unconscious mind" (p. 281).

Schore (2012) elaborates on Affective Regulation Therapy (ART), which as he describes it, relies to a large extent on facilitating and managing experiences of stressful affects activated by the treatment relationship. Specifically, longstanding dissociations that have kept painful affects sequestered break down and old traumas are reenacted. However, in the new relational context, the empathically resonating analyst, being a coparticipant in a "regulated" enactment, works to maintain a right-hemisphere–to–right-hemisphere connection so that previously overwhelming traumatic feelings can be integrated into the patient's emotional life. Ultimately, Schore believes that this form of right-hemisphere psychotherapy changes brain structure and functioning:

> Effective therapy can positively alter the developmental trajectory of the deep right hemisphere and facilitate the integration between cortical and subcortical right hemisphere systems. The enhanced interconnectivity allows for an increased complexity of defenses of the emotional right hemisphere, coping strategies for regulating stressful affect that are more flexible and adaptive than pathological dissociation. This in turn enhances the further maturation of the right hemisphere core of the self and its central involvement in patterns of affect that integrate a sense of self across state transitions, thereby allowing for a continuity of inner experience.
>
> (Schore, 2012, p. 106)

In other words, Schore argues that effective psychotherapy produces massive rewiring of the brain that undoes the damage of a traumatic early childhood. Most analysts would want this to be true, but I think we should be cautious about asserting that analytic psychotherapy can reliably accomplish such sweeping psychological and behavioral changes, not to mention fundamental physical alterations of "deep" brain structures. To support this claim Schore cites a *JAMA* editorial by R. M. Glass (2008), who states, citing various research findings, that "psychotherapy affects regional blood flow, neurotransmitter metabolism, gene expression and persistent modification in synaptic plasticity" (p. 1589). In a review of this research by Kay and Kay (2011), the authors are clear that these physical changes in the brain seem to be associated with *various* forms of psychotherapy (analytic and nonanalytic) and educational approaches. However, Schore fails to note that these findings are more complicated than the quote from Glass suggests; often they are preliminary, their implications as yet unclear. How brain alterations happen, and what the consequences are, we can't say for sure. This certainly bears looking into, but Schore is jumping the gun when he claims more specific brain effects and outcomes, let alone advances the idea that analytic psychotherapy can undo developmental damage incurred during the earliest phases of brain maturation. In a sentence not quoted by Schore, Glass is more cautious: "Whether such findings [physical changes resulting from psychotherapy] might eventually lead to improved ways to assess psychotherapies or drug therapies, or to match particular psychotherapies or combination therapies to fundamental patient needs, is an exciting but *uncertain* possibility" (Glass 2008, p. 1589).

Despite these uncertainties, I believe Schore's research and integrative efforts have important implications for a population of challenging clients who suffer early abuse and neglect during the first two years of life. These patients suffer from deficits in right-hemisphere structuralization and functioning. Their problems are not due to a disorder in creativity, but an incapacity for secure attachment and cohesive self-structure. The goal of treatment is to provide an experience which helps to address developmental deficits, repair and/or augment self-disorders, and provide opportunities for improved interpersonal relatedness. Putting right-hemisphere attachment deficits and needs at the forefront of our clinical understanding and interventions is essential with these people, and Schore's work is enormously helpful in this regard. However, once again, the capacity for creative living will not be the concern for these patients, at least in the early phases of treatment, and perhaps never.

That being said, what are the implications of Schore's study for the practice of psychotherapy with the general population of patients with whom the issue of attachment is diverse and its impact variable? Most patients who enter treatment do not suffer from primary attachment disorders (let alone one early childhood relational traumas); more often the attachment problems they complain of results from the impact of later traumas, adjustment issues, situational stresses, or old-fashioned neurotic conflicts. In these instances, targeting attachment would not be central to the treatment. For these people (the vast majority of our patients) attachment is important but is best viewed as a background issue, not the main focus of the treatment. These patients struggle with psychological problems which restrict their response to living and compel them into modes of feeling and acting which are repetitive, ineffective and a source of pain. These therapies require a balanced brain approach. Once the stress that has brought the patient into treatment is addressed with some right-brain–to–right-brain work, the treatment may soon turn to a largely verbal exploration of fantasy, defense, and transference.

Rather than qualifying his model, which is based on the study of a limited population of patients traumatized in early infancy, Schore extrapolates the findings and his hypotheses about adult pathology and treatment to a range of other clinical conditions and to the practice of psychotherapy in general. Characterizing psychotherapy as a right-hemisphere–to–right-hemisphere communication treatment, he elevates his very useful understanding of early attachment disorders and their treatment to the status of a general psychology in which the right hemisphere is dominant and the left hemisphere, along with the use of language, is viewed as, at best, secondary.

Central to my critique is my belief that Schore's understanding of the right hemisphere's role in creativity is also a problem. He argued that the seat of creativity lies in the right hemisphere's special abilities and attitudes – I do not think this is correct. Referring to the work of Ansburg and Hill (2003) Schore argues that "creative" thinkers (right hemisphere predominant) compared to "analytic" thinkers (left hemisphere predominant) are:

> More likely to produce no consciously primed solutions, gather information using diffuse instead of focused attentional processes that occur beneath awareness, sample a wider range of environmental input, and generate innovative connections when they unwittingly encounter a trigger in the environment.

Schore then quotes Ansberg and Hill (2003): "Instead of relying solely on explicit memory processes, creative individuals may be able to take a better advantage of their implicit memory processes" (2003, p. 1149). The important word in this quote is "solely" which indicates that truly creative individuals rely on both explicit and implicit thinking when doing creative work. Several recent studies (De Dreu *et al.*, 2012; Wiley and Jarosz, 2012) show that creativity involves the capacity for flexibility of attentional focus such that the person is able to both direct and relax attention making use of both left-brain and right-brain capacities when solving problems or achieving a new insight. Too much or too little focus can inhibit creativity; a balance between the two is ideal. I would argue (and this is supported by McGilchrist) that creativity requires the participation of both the implicit and the explicit. The notion of relying primarily on one or the other mode destroys, or at least greatly restricts, creative thinking. Ultimately the right brain (largely unconscious and embedded) is unable to step back from a situation or a problem in order to examine it and apply new abstract approaches. In this case being embedded, relying primarily on intuition, affect and unconscious processes can lead to paralysis and confusion, rather than insight and creativity. Effective creative thinking in psychotherapy requires the ability to distance oneself, apply learned knowledge and professionally acquired abstractions (e.g. ideas, concepts, formulations, leaned techniques, values) while at the same time being able to access and use right-hemisphere attitudes of intuition, grasping the gestalt, and defocusing to augment the left-hemisphere's analysis. From this perspective, creativity is a *process* which optimally involves the particular abilities and strengths of both hemispheres. Once again, we see dialectic at the heart of the creative process.

Nonetheless, Allan Schore exhorts therapists to eschew verbal interpretation and go with one's feelings and communicate body to body, brain to brain, without the stifling restriction of consciousness and language. The problem is we cannot silence the left hemisphere (nor, as we will see, should we) – what would the right hemisphere think without the left-hemisphere's words? Part of the problem is Schore's tendency to view language as primarily a left hemisphere function. Iain McGilchrist points out that language functions are distributed across both left and right brains, and like everything else, have different meanings in the two hemispheres. Each uses language differently, and different aspects of it stand out in the use that each hemisphere makes of language. While things like syntax and vocabulary are housed in the left brain, the right hemisphere makes understanding the words possible, as well as decoding language's emotional significance and less-rational aspects. The right hemisphere humanizes language. But without the left hemisphere, the right hemisphere would be speechless, lacking the tools necessary to make sense of the world or of the self. McGilchrist's findings also imply that language is a tool for the exploration of the unconscious. In fact, the right-brain's crucial role in giving emotional meaning to language supports the idea that the use of language in psychotherapy is a crucial active agent in the communication that goes on between the brains of patients and therapists (a point Schore is aware of but does not elaborate). Without the left hemisphere the right hemisphere is mute, a cauldron of feeling and impressions that cannot be given form (the id?). With the help of the left hemisphere, the right hemisphere is given the capacity to use symbols, which, imbuing these abstractions with passion, feeling, humor, and the like, make human relationships and human culture possible. I would argue that the only way analysts can manage and make use of the nonverbal, affectively dysregulated experience of enactment is to mobilize the resources of the left hemisphere (equipped perhaps with the memory of Schore's books) to join forces with the emotional right hemisphere, to work through and make sense of the (until then) unconscious clinical processes. After all, the power of psychoanalysis has been to bring language and the body together in a dynamic tension that allows the work to get done. The role of the therapist is to assist the patient in bringing left hemisphere and right hemisphere back on line as an effectively functioning system, in which diversity, connectedness, interdependence, and the drive for adaptation create the conditions for creativity.

While I agree with Schore that psychoanalysis has overemphasized left-brain functioning, it seems necessary to inquire how we can more effectively balance left and right functions so that both are included in our models of psychopathology and health. Most important, we need to better understand how our two brains collaborate in effective clinical treatment. Most psychotherapies including, I would assume, Art, consist of regular, structured, familiar, and conversation-based sessions. Affects are regulated by this structure but also by our use of language. These left-hemisphere aspects do inhibit and contain affective processes, helping to establish and maintain a stable baseline for treatment. Schore is right to point out that in affectively dysregulated experiences language is not as effective as responsiveness and "deep" contact. However, the therapist's ability to think through the process and mobilize left hemisphere resources may be essential to his or her ability to figure out what to do. Surrender to a traumatic state of feeling and being can be risky for both patient and therapist. The left-hemisphere's ability to coolly break the situation down, analyze and even apply some theory to the problem is frequently necessary. After all, except in instances of severe brain injury or such traumatic states as Schore describes, both brains function simultaneously and should not be viewed apart from one another. The therapist must retain analytical skill and the capacity to access language. This is a function of the left hemisphere.

Unfortunately Schore did not elaborate on the unique functions of the left hemisphere, and his thesis that psychotherapy is primarily a right-brain-to-right-hemisphere relationship strongly suggests that the left brain is not relevant to the psychotherapeutic process. However, if we look at the work of Iain McGilchrist, we see that the left hemisphere plays an essential role in psychoanalytic forms of therapy. Most importantly an appreciation of the left hemisphere's relationship with the right sheds light on the creative function of interpretation and working through in analysis.

McGilchrist argued that the left hemisphere has a fundamentally different attitude toward the world and the self from the right hemisphere. The left is the domain of consciousness and language, rather than having a receptive posture, the left is assertive and grasping, seeking to break down experience into manageable and familiar parts, creating linear models which help it to exert control and mastery. Abstracting from experience and creating lifeless symbolic system equivalents of vital experience is the left hemisphere's forte. McGilchrist wrote:

> Clarity and fixity are added by the left hemisphere, which is what makes it possible for us to control, manipulate or use the world. For this, attention is directed and focused; the wholeness is broken into parts; the implicit is unpacked; language becomes the instrument of serial analysis; things are categorized and become familiar. Affect is set aside and superseded by cognitive abstraction; the conscious mind is brought to bear on the situation; thoughts are sent to the left hemisphere for expression in words . . . This enables us to have knowledge and bring the world into resolution, but it leaves what it knows denatured and decontexualized. The left hemisphere is never the end point, always a staging point. It is a useful department to send things for processing, but things only have meaning once again when they are returned to the right hemisphere.
>
> (p. 195)

> The left hemisphere seems to play a crucial role in determining what comes into being; it is part of the process of creation. Applying linear, sequential analysis forces the implicit into explicitness, and brings clarity; this is crucial in helping bring about an aspect of what is there. But in doing so the whole is lost.
>
> (p. 207)

McGilchrist argues that, taken alone, each hemisphere is incapable of sustained creativity. For example, despite the right hemisphere's strength in the areas of implicit cognition and affect, fluidity, intuition, and direct connection to the body and physical reality, it can also be constrained by these qualities. As McGilchrist explains, the right brain:

> Cannot sufficiently, on its own, disengage itself from "the natural viewpoint". The "too, too solid flesh" of everydayness hangs about it. It therefore all too easily lapses: it is constrained by everyday reality, and its viability depends on not being unnaturally ruptured from the lived world.
>
> (p. 225)

Right-hemisphere self-experience is embedded in a social reality which is in one sense vivid, passionate and alive, but is also controlled by affect, is unconscious and highly constrained by the constant demands of physical and social life. Hence the life of the right hemisphere is essential to human connectedness and emotional engagement with others. However, contrary to Schore's belief, the right hemisphere is not inherently creative, although it does possess capacities which, activated by interaction with the left hemisphere, contribute important elements to the creative process. But it cannot (and does not want to) do this creative work alone.

The left hemisphere's strengths are its ability to separate, to abstract and break experience down into pieces, to apply ideas and develop systems to make sense of and control reality. The left hemisphere is aware, practical, useful and, most importantly, rational. However, these capacities also alienate the person from the world, drain vitality out of lived experience, impose order onto an inherently ambiguous and rich reality, reduce flexibility and constrain the person's openness to life. Left to its own devices the left hemisphere would be trapped in a solipsistic world of its own highly abstracted fantasies, isolated from others, and incapable of managing the complexity and ambiguity of the social world. The left hemisphere depends on the right hemisphere to give life to experience, to negotiate social relationships, and allow for thoughts and feelings which are responsive and engaged with other people. In summary, the right hemisphere needs the left hemisphere in order to step back and think about the world, and the right hemisphere needs the left to feel connected and to manage the passionate and implicit aspects of emotional and social life – the outcome of this dialectic is creative living. McGilchrist describes this process as follows:

> Thought begins and ends in the right hemisphere, passing through the necessary staging post of the left hemisphere where it is put into serial sentences. This follows a typical pattern in the way the hemispheres relate: the origins and end lie in the right hemisphere's world, but it is greatly enriched by what the left hemisphere can "unpack" along the way. That middle stage, of making the parts temporarily explicit, before they are once more reintegrated into the

> whole, is crucial. Yet it cannot be the endpoint. It is like learning a piece of music: first you are drawn to play it as a whole; then you break it down into bits and practice certain passages, and analyze harmonic transitions, and so on; but in the performance all that must one again be set ruthlessly aside, or the result would be disastrous.
>
> (p. 255)

All human things can be thought of as a product of this fruitful tension.

The creative analyst takes a position *vis-à-vis* the patient which is between the right and left hemisphere. As we learn from Schore, the implicit, relational aspects of the analytic relationship provides an empathic, holding environment in which deep aspects of self-experience and relatedness are confirmed and responded to. The analyst's right hemisphere, guided by empathy and attention to shared affective exchanges, responds to the patient's right hemisphere providing clinically useful experiences which can address therapeutic needs arising from developmental failures and traumas. However, as we learn from McGilchrist, the left brain has a role here as well. The analyst works with the patient to use attention, analysis and language to separate out and highlight aspects of experience, hitherto unconscious, and by means of words and the drive to adapt and gain control, a new understanding is developed and a new vision of experience becomes the topic of discussion and analysis.

But if interpretations remain only as words, abstractions of experience, then accurate and insightful as they may be, they remain clinically useless unless the analyst and patient reintroduce what is "understood" to the right-brain. The result is a synthesis of left and right. This process involves grounding the insight in unconscious experience through the linking of interpretation to affect, body experiences and implicit dimensions of relatedness. In addition, the new conscious understanding is placed in context and reintegrated into the wholesome structure of right hemisphere experiencing and most importantly, of the self. It is also important to understand that this process of back and forth, the reverberative quality of right- and left-brain communication is ongoing and characterizes all aspects of everyday human psychological life. In this light the analytic relationship is an especially potent tool in this process. Most important, the analyst's engagement with both sides of the patient's brain allows for a form of collaboration between the hemispheres which goes against design. In fact, McGilchrist points out that the radically different nature and attitudes of each hemisphere lead to a situation where neither can know what is happening within the other. The corpus callosum, which links and separates the hemispheres' major function is to inhibit activities and reduce the potential for sharing. The analyst uses his or her understanding of the whole patient (a right hemisphere function) to understand and analyze, formulating interpretations which are verbalized both to the patient's left brain and then reintroduces with an infusion of affect to the right, and then back again to the left; a process, which can be very rapid, broken up into microseconds in some cases and repeated endlessly. The results are the ongoing elaboration of new understandings (left brain) which are then grounded and reintegrated into an embodied, emotionally rich and highly contextualized sense of being (right hemisphere). This is the dynamic of the creative brain, which is structurally organized to bring about the potential for something new. I believe that psychoanalysis is uniquely designed to leverage this creative process for clinical benefit, not through alignment with one side (as Schore argues) but through a balanced and flexible engagement with both hemispheres, an understanding of the special attitudes possessed by each, and a dynamic sensitivity to the way the attitudes of each hemisphere can be converted into the life world of the other, enriching the meaning and value of the whole. The following is an example:

> John is a bright 30 year old man who I have seen in weekly psychotherapy for 2 years. Much of our work had centered on his problems with his job, most importantly his tendency to experience his boss as a judgmental and rejecting father figure. His biological father had been a distant, authoritarian and alcoholic figure in his early life, so the transfer of this old relationship to the workplace was not hard for him to understand. We successfully identified the fearful emotions and fantasies which inhibited him in his dealings with the boss, and some progress had been made in being more assertive.
>
> During the second year John began to miss some appointments because of his commitments to a professional organization in which he had been given a leadership role. He called to cancel when necessary but at times I was notified late, or at the last minute. I found myself becoming annoyed and asked him about the late notifications.
>
> "I guess I could try harder. Sometimes I don't think of it. Sort of like with my boss."
>
> "I'm like your boss?"
>
> "No . . . not at all. But I mean I sometimes don't tell him what I am doing. He's called me on that at times."
>
> "Perhaps in the way I'm calling you on it."
>
> "You're a lot nicer."
>
> "Maybe, but you have some worries that I might be critical."
>
> "OK . . . Maybe the father-thing again."
>
> "Again?"
>
> "Well, I don't know. But we have found out how I react to men in authority as if they were like my father – you know, cold and critical."
>
> "OK . . . That may be helpful. What does it feel like when you have to call me? When you know that another obligation will keep you from session."
>
> "Well . . . I get a bit confused. I tend to procrastinate. I don't like it either. The more I wait the worse it gets."
>
> "What gets?"
>
> "I imagine your gonna get more and more pissed at me."
>
> "And you feel more frightened . . . as I become more like him in your mind."

"Yes. You are him to me and I am sure you won't put up with me and then I am sure you will hate me."

"The way you felt your father hated you."

"Yeah . . . I feel like that time I had been playing baseball with my friends. I was on a roll so it was dark when I got home. He was livid, I knew it. So I waited outside on the stoop, crying. I knew I should just go in and get it over with, but I couldn't. I can feel it now. My whole body shook. I was terrified."

John looked up at me, fear in his eyes.

"And he did let me have it. But you know it was better to have it out in the end. It was worse out on that stoop not knowing."

John's "insight" into the source of his avoidance of me was the beginning of a useful transference interpretation and working-through process. His initial statement that the late cancelations had something to do with the "father-thing" was a piece of left hemisphere work. He was able to put into words a conceptualization which linked the new behavior into something already known and familiar, but in a new context. This is an important function of the left brain, which takes the buzzing confusion of everyday life and seeks consistency and order mostly through familiar ideas and words. But the insight would have been useless without our transfer of the left hemisphere, verbal insight into right hemisphere affective experience. By connecting the idea of the "father-thing" to old experiences with his father, and especially affective states evoked by childhood fantasies of criticism and punishment, we were able to transform the lifeless idea into deeply felt, physically vivid memories of his father. This is a fairly familiar example of interpretive work, but it illustrates how we commonly act as liaisons between the two hemispheres, helping to convert the left hemisphere's cool insights into a passionate and psychologically rich recognition of previously unconscious fantasies. The result leads to truly new and creative developments in the clinical process which would not have been possible if only one hemisphere had been engaged in the work.

Can we identify specific techniques which encourage and facilitate the conversion process between left- and right-brain attitudes? For example what does the analyst add to the left hemisphere verbal interpretation to help convert it into a right hemisphere experience, thus making the insight relevant and useful to the more emotional, relationally embedded self? Let me offer several suggestions regarding working with fantasies such as John's "father-thing". First, the analyst and patient should elaborate the sensory components of the fantasies; second, encourage the expression of the affects associated with the fantasies; third, link these fantasies and feelings to memories of being with the boss and with the analyst; fourth, put everything in context, of the job, the patient's family of origin, the transference; fifth, encourage an empathic attitudes toward the self which means encourage the patient to decenter and reflect on his state of mind and feeling during these meetings with father figures. There will then be a point where a detail or dimension of the session will be highlighted and taken out of context to examine and understand. "I wonder if these experiences with your boss and me are similar to some of those humiliating childhood encounters with your father when he was drunk." In this way the analytic process reverberates between the worlds and attitudes of the left and right hemispheres as a continually unfolding creative process.

Conclusion

Recent developments in brain research, especially our understanding of the special nature and dynamics of brain hemisphere differentiation, not only help us to know more about the neuropsychology of mental life, but also have valuable things to contribute to contemporary psychoanalytic practice. In this chapter I have pointed out what I believe to be the limitations of Allen Schore's model of right hemisphere predominance in psychotherapy. We have examined how Iain McGilchrist's work sheds light on the way in which implicit and explicit dimensions of right- and left-hemisphere functioning can inform psychoanalytic practice, most importantly the way in which verbal interventions and non-verbal embodied interventions can enhance and amplify each other. Going beyond the reductionistic model of Allen Schore's focus on right-hemisphere dynamics in treatment, we have seen how both the verbal and non-verbal can reverberate and mutually enhance each other. In addition understanding the dynamics of the asymmetrical brain also adds a dimension of non-relationality to contemporary discourse. Asserting the contribution of the left hemisphere to psychological health and creativity may not be popular, but as we have seen, the left-brain's very inhumanity allows people to step out of the restrictions of social and physical life, benefiting from the disruptive power of words and reason. I believe that this special dynamic of the balanced brain model allows psychoanalytic approaches to take full advantage of the potential of the creative brain.

Chapter 4

Aesthetic interaction

(with Carol M. Press, Ed.D)*

In Chapter 3, we discussed the ongoing dialectic between the implicit, relationally based attitude of the right hemisphere and the explicit, depersonalized attitudes of the left. However, it is important to note that the right hemisphere is the primary means of communication between artist and artwork, and between analyst and analysand. As Schore stresses, the most powerful communication occurs between the right brain of the analyst and the right brain of the analysand. Although the left may "make sense" of these connections, give them words and challenge the right brain to "think" about the feeling of what happens, it is the right brain which connects us to each other, unconsciously, body to body, gesture to gesture. At the heart of these relational connections is aesthetics, the felt quality of our experience of living. Generally we think of aesthetics as a dimension of our experience of the world. As we view a dazzling sunset, a quiet wooded grove, the David, or the Cathedral of Chartes, we remark on how beautiful or sublime the world can be. But aesthetics is a quality of experience itself not just of objects, and thus the term can apply not only to outward perception, but also to the quality of self-experience. Most important, an aesthetic sense of our being-in-the-world, especially the relation of self to other, is fundamental to who we feel we are, and is basic to our sense of the quality of our lives and our emotional well-being.

Part I

Carol M. Press

Our aesthetic sense of self and our capacity for empathy are intimately intertwined, informing self-experience from infancy onward. Gilbert J. Rose (2004) in his book *Between Couch and Piano: Music, Art, Psychoanalysis and Neuroscience* reminds us that the beginnings of "aesthetic responsiveness . . . lie in the nonverbal emotional rapport and empathy of the earliest infant-parent interplay" (p. 1). Simultaneously, empathic bonds and our sense of the aesthetic are inherent to the

*Carol M. Press, Ed.D is on the faculty at UC Santa Barbara. Author of *The Dancing Self: Creativity, Modern Dance, Self Psychology, and Transformative Education* (Hampton Press, 2002).

early relational interactions between parent and baby. Significantly, empathic bonds embrace distinctive aesthetic qualities as the infant learns through discerning patterns of shape, time, intensity, and affect arousal (Beebe and Lachmann, 2002; Stern, 1985), while influencing and engaging relationships.

Daniel Stern's (1985) description of vitality affects poignantly captures qualitative dimensions of experience: "surging, fading away, fleeting, explosive, crescendo, decrescendo, bursting, drawn out, and so on" (p. 54). These vitality affects filter and flavor subjective exchanges, commingling emotional response and aesthetic qualities. Consequently, tending to one's baby entails actions imbued with qualitative aesthetic experience. Stern identifies the direct connection between such early infant-parent interactions and the creating and partaking of art as an adult:

> Abstract dance and music are examples par excellence of the expressiveness of vitality affects . . . The choreographer is most often trying to express a way of feeling, not a specific content of feeling . . . Like dance for the adult, the social world experienced by the infant is primarily one of vitality affects before it is a world of formal acts.
>
> (pp. 56–57)

Through early aesthetic qualitative exchanges we develop feelings and values about experiences and relationships that continually influence our lives. George Hagman (2005a) in his book. *Aesthetic Experience* describes these emotional bonds as:

> value affects . . . These affects reflect the personal significance and value . . . Most importantly these value affects are communicative – they convey how one feels about the other. Affects such as love have internal references, but they are ineluctably tied to the other – "I love" is only half of the equation – "I love you" is a value affect . . . Within the relational matrix these affects mutually communicate the experience of shared value.

Vitality affects, value affects and empathic interactions all have a qualitative aesthetic base, endowed with experiences of shape, time, energy, sensation and feeling, propelling us through our lives.

Traditionally, our aesthetic responsiveness is perceived as our sense of beauty. Implicit is dichotomy; implicit in our sense of beauty is our sense of ugliness, that which subjectively fractures beauty. (See Hagman, 2005a, for an extensive psychoanalytic treatment of beauty and ugliness.) We speak of beauty and ugliness as if they are qualities of external objects. We exclaim: "That is beautiful!" or "That is ugly!" However, our sense of the beautiful and the ugly are external frames upon which we hang our aesthetic values and ideals originally derived from early life. In *The Dancing Self* I elaborate on the significance for engaging art:

> The seeds for our aesthetic endeavors are . . . the early relations between infant and caregiver . . . These relations, unless damaged, carry the ideal bliss of the pleasure humans intrinsically find in their offspring . . . The beginnings of intimacy and aesthetic pleasure are planted through the healthy idealization inherent in these relations. In our creative endeavors we elaborate on these initial experiences, giving them texture, weaving them into new configurations now touched and expanded by the lived experiences of our lives. We are connected to our past, integrated with our present, propelled with hope for our future. If successful, we feel whole. We partake of, and are nourished by, the functioning aesthetic selfobject.
>
> (Press, 2002, p. 100)

Consequently, from infancy onward, interactions that feel good can permeate desire – a sense of beauty; the actions that feel bad can permeate aversion – a sense of ugliness; hence, when a driving motivation, a psychological aesthetic sense of ugliness through relationship may penetrate an aversive motivational system (Lichtenberg, 1988, 1989; Lichtenberg *et al.*, 1992, 1996). Of course, in pathology negative affects and forms of relating can become part of our daily repertoire of experience, trailing us throughout our lives. Embedded in our relationships, in health and pathology, are our qualitative aesthetic sense of beauty and ugliness, which inform our empathic engagements.

How does an aesthetic sense of self inform the co-construction of empathy? Our aesthetic sense of self is often non-conscious and an important building block of procedural knowledge and memory. Frank Lachmann (2004) in his talk "On the co-construction of empathy" describes procedural memory derived from early infant and caregiver interactions such as "cross-modal transfer, rhythm coordination, state sharing in terms of action, feeling, or proprioception". Lachmann makes clear that procedural memory is non-conscious but not repressed. Indeed, we remember how to tie our shoes without having to consciously contemplate the act. Some may typically tie their shoes languidly, while others do so with determined speed and efficiency. Either way we tie our shoes with an aesthetic sensibility. Additionally, the Boston Change Study Group (Stern *et al.,* 1998), capturing the significance of vitality affects and value affects, highlights interpersonal events as procedures. According to Lachmann (2004) these include: "how to relate to a baby, how to flirt, how to have fun, how to dance, how to enter the subjective state of another person and how to signal one's readiness to respond to another person entering our private life; as actions these are in part organized on a procedural level". We emphasize that, as actions, these are in part organized on an aesthetic level.

Lachmann highlights that such procedural memories are the precursors for our co-constructed empathic relationships, and that additionally, for empathy to come to fruition, conscious cognitive understanding is necessary. Aesthetic procedural memories become integrated with conscious cognition to create the possibility of empathic bonds. Consequently, aesthetic quality conjoins with content to permit our deepest empathic relations, and ultimately sustains our connection to the arts.

Lachmann's discussion of an experiment done with students at Barnard demonstrates the importance of such qualitative aesthetic experience. The students wore throat microphones that recorded only the rhythmic patterns of their speech (i.e. when someone was speaking, stopped speaking, and then started speaking again) but no conversational content. Afterwards, students stated with whom they would want to have dinner. Choices were made not on content, nor how long they spoke with one another, but a matching of vocal rhythmic patterns that were best coordinated. The best sense of relationship was not based on what was said but indeed how it was said on a procedural and aesthetic level. The capacity to expect constructive relations develops from an aesthetic sense of self.

This is congruous with "something more" than interpretation discussed by the Daniel Stern and the Boston Change Group (Stern *et al.*, 1998). Alan Kindler, in his paper (2010) "Improvisation and spontaneity in psychoanalysis" discusses their contribution:

> The Boston Group (Stern *et al.*, 1998) has written extensively on the "something more" than interpretation which contributes to change in the therapeutic relationship. Drawing heavily on developmental research, they suggest that therapeutic change occurs at the level of "implicit relational knowing", the procedurally encoded rules of how relationships are conducted such as what to expect of the other and what is expected of oneself . . . The patient and therapist may be exploring their relationship in the verbal mode. This takes place in the foreground. At the same time, in the background, is a parallel process of non-verbal interaction regulated by the rules of "implicit relational knowing" which govern the "shared implicit relationship". In the background of all relationships, they suggest, is a complex realm of nonverbal communication governed by the rules of how we are together, what we expect of one another and what we know about each other's expectations at any point in time.

Steven Knoblauch (2000) in his book *The Musical Edge of Therapeutic Dialogue* demonstrates his use of tone, pitch, rhythm and improvisational turn-taking in the analytic situation to comprehend and influence the dynamic relations orchestrated between himself and his patients. Frank Lachmann (2001) in his article "Words and music" highlights the importance of such co-constructed dialogues:

> As we listen to music or to the associations of analysands, our accompanying rhythms are likely to alter, as we mold our rhythms to the rhythms of the other and they mold their rhythms to ours. In this rhythmic interaction, our own repertoire of rhythms will increase. The beat of our music and that of our analysands can be coordinated or syncopated, but, one hopes, we do not get too far off the beat.
>
> (p. 174)

Rose, in his book *Between Couch and Piano* (2004) includes a musician's articulation of feeling out of sync aesthetically with the therapist. This dyad is off to a "bad 'musical' start" which has gotten "off the beat":

> I can't locate him as a person and feel like it's a space of theatre (the theatre of therapist and patient) . . . I imagined him on stage as a musician. I believe I would be really put off. . . .
>
> It all reminds me of the feeling I get (and other musicians, too) when I play chamber music with a new person: he/she may be a great musician, but if the chemistry isn't right and the energy and sound colors don't match, it just doesn't work.
>
> I think what bothered me most was a lack of smooth transition between this guy's silences and his talking. The language – the sound – did not meet the silence. So I wasn't able to perceive an organic rhythm of breath etc. – and the silence (and the talking) didn't mean much. The silences seemed empty and the sounds forced, that is, not enough tension or too much.
>
> (pp. 9–10)

Unfortunately, this patient does not experience an empathic attunement between himself and therapist on an aesthetic level. Most importantly, Rose (2004) asserts that this level of communication is pertinent in all clinical work: "Nonverbal affect embodied in abstract art like music may need to be assigned a status alongside the established importance of narrative fantasy, free association, interpretation and insight" (p. xxix). The views of Rose, Knoblauch, Lachmann, Stern and his colleagues help expand our understanding of empathy to include nonverbal aesthetic qualities of interaction as fundamental to any co-constructed relationship. David Shaddock in his article "The opening of the field: Thoughts on the poetics of psychoanalytic treatment" examines the therapeutic relationship from the aesthetics of language itself. Shaddock takes the lens of poetry, its creative use of metaphor, image, sound, rhythm and form, and explores "both a heightened sense of meaning and the lulling trance of sound and rhythm – and the way one listens to both the content and the nonverbal aspects of patients' communication". Indeed, we believe the therapeutic situation can be examined as an aesthetic medium through which to engage the dynamics of a clinical creative process fueled by each individual's embodied aesthetic self-experience.

Analysts who highlight findings from infant research (Beebe and Lachmann, 2002; Lichtenberg, 1988, 1989; Lichtenberg *et al.*, 1992, 1996; Stern, 1985), describe the development of subjectivity and intersubjectivity through early infant and caregiver interactions. Such interactions are based upon discerning, engaging, creating, organizing, and integrating patterns of time, shape, space, affect, and arousal. These early experiences cross sensory modalities. Ellen Dissanayake (2000) in her book, *Art and Intimacy*, describes the cross-modal aesthetic exchange of "baby talk":

> From the first weeks, in all cultures . . . a mother's vocalizations to the baby and her facial expressions, gestures, and head and body movements are exaggerated – made clear and rhythmic. Babies in turn respond with corresponding sounds, expressions, and movements of their own, and over the first months a mutual multimedia ritual performance emerges and develops. Exquisitely satisfying to both participants, it inundates both mother and baby with a special pleasure that is all the more powerful because it is not just felt alone . . . but is mirrored or shared.
>
> (p. 29)

Eventually such interactions translate into the aesthetic formal properties shared by all the arts such as time, shape, space, energy, rhythm, pulse, contrast and so forth. These aesthetic elements constitute a language for ongoing dialogues of our co-constructed relationships and potential for individuation and mutuality. They constitute the profound nourishment shared culturally of the aesthetic through the making and partaking of art.

Aesthetic tendencies and signatures are powerful elements of our emotional and psychological lives. Artists, perhaps indicative of their capacities for fluidity within self-organization, possess heightened accessibility and sensitivity to modalities and aesthetic qualities of experience; this procedural knowledge forms the bedrock of their talents, their aesthetic languages. In *The Dancing Self* (2002) I elaborate extensively on dancers' relationship and engagement with sensation as the source of their expressive language and talents. Through their relationship to sensation, dancers spontaneously evolve aesthetic signatures that bear a cornerstone of their aesthetic beginnings. From here dancers dynamically search to elaborate their aesthetic signatures and to explore and develop artistically in new directions. We all have aesthetic signatures that sign our procedural and psychological core. Some clinicians (Knoblauch, 2000; Rose, 2004) now suggest the importance of heightening their empathic expectations to include these aesthetic qualitative sensitivities. Self-awareness and self-empathy regarding one's own aesthetic nonverbal communication, and the capacity to attune to another's aesthetic, becomes a significant aspect of empathic engagement, clinical theory and practice.

The role of creative engagement, expressive of an aesthetic sense of self, may become significant within the clinical situation. Often, experiences of past trauma are perceived as a main motivation to express one's aesthetic sense of self through the making of art in the search for repair and restoration or some aspect of self-cohesion. What is implicit in this idea is that the foundational motivation for art-making is a "forward edge" move (Tolpin, 2002) dynamically connected to joy and healthy development, which is then brought into the service of repair. This move can be very apparent in the artist. In the article, "The musician and the creative process", George Hagman (2005b) comments upon his case of Paul, a once nationally recognized cellist who came to treatment experiencing serious inhibitions in regards to his performance and creativity:

> His talent appeared to transcend the turmoil in his childhood home, bringing him back to an early perhaps fantasized time of harmony and comfort . . . a place of wonder and vitality that he could return to as needed.

Paul's talents connect him to his forward edge development: consequently, the vitalization of joyful self-experience makes art available and useful in Paul's restoration from trauma.

Unfortunately, for a number of years, Paul lost this joyful connection and his sense of self and art making suffered. Paul poignantly discusses the period in his life when he gave up music: "I hated myself. I had lost everything." Paul's performance restoration occurs when he embodies his aesthetic sense of self through self-mastery and the joy of expressive efficacy. Paul tells George:

> Music really has to do with your body. For example, I realized that I had been tightening my fingers in a certain way, that effected my playing, and when I made a slight change I noticed a big difference . . . You play music through your body. You have to relax and give yourself over to it.

The reintegration of this joy sustains Paul in overcoming performance difficulties. When Paul becomes aware of his procedural knowledge and his non-conscious mode of playing, he alters his tendency to tighten his fingers. Self-esteem is restored through expressive self-assertion.

An assertive/exploratory motivational system (Lichtenberg, 1988, 1989; Lichtenberg *et al.*, 1992, 1996) leads to competency, self-mastery, and efficacy joy. Ultimately, this reinforces and renews the motivation for self-assertion and exploration. As an artist I feel a visceral connection to this depiction; I have read no other description that so psychologically and experientially captures for me the joy of creative engagement – the sustenance necessary to traverse the trials and tribulations of the creative process. The hoped for expectation of self-mastery reinforces self-experience to first encounter and then engage ambiguity, an essential challenge in creative work that often brings about experiences of anxiety. Such self-experience is grounded in aesthetically endowed procedural memory.

Artists appear to have a heightened sensitivity to connect through an aesthetic sense of self and procedural memory. Artists take procedural memory and bring it forth as aesthetic expression and through such activity build empathic connections. In *The Dancing Self* I discuss Kohut's (1987, p. 271) comparison of empathy to the aesthetic partaking of theater:

> Audience members open themselves to resonate with the characters portrayed on stage. The result can be deeply moving and engrossing. But the audience never forgets that they are in a theater, that the people on stage are actors. The audience understands and imagines the life displayed on stage, experiences an empathic reverberation with the events, emotions, and psychological states.
>
> (Press, 2002, p. 44)

This capacity for empathic imagination is rooted in our development of procedural memory fueled with vitality affects and aesthetic qualities. According to Dissanayake (2000):

> We respond cross-modally and emotionally to the swoop and exuberance of a dance movement, the sense of hesitation or resignation and defeat in an actor's gesture, or the thick guttural innuendo in a jazz singer's voice, usually before recognizing or assigning symbolic "meaning" to the dance style of the spoken or unsung words.
>
> (p. 147)

The precursors for empathy, discussed by Lachmann, evolve over the course of our lifetimes to enhance and develop our capacity for the aesthetic and for relationships with others. Kohut in *How Does Analysis Cure?* (1984) and his essay "On empathy" (1981/1991) captures this evolution in the notion of a developmental line of empathy. He describes the little boy in the park, wandering further away from his mother than usual to exuberantly chase the pigeons. He looks back at his mother to see her pride in his more independent accomplishment and his joy. Kohut (1981/1991) claims:

> A low form of empathy, a body-close form of empathy, expressed in holding and touching and smelling, is now expressed only in facial expressions and perhaps later in words, "I'm proud of you, my boy."
>
> (p. 533)

The early procedural bodily experiences are now cross-modally communicated on a more sophisticated level. The precursors of empathy progress into a developmental line of empathy and, we suggest, simultaneously into a developmental line of our aesthetic sense of self.

My life and work as a dancer and choreographer feels profoundly nourished by such elemental relational concepts. My psychological task in life has been dominated by this journey. Many years ago, on the evening before I was to meet my new therapist, I had a dream that I was walking through the countryside. A gentle soothing breeze was blowing. I was dressed in drab nondescript clothing. I came across a farmhouse and a lovely young woman had placed upon an outside clothesline many leotards. The breeze had dried them. They were ready for wear. In my dream I watched the motion of the leotards as they danced through the air, a symphony of rhythm. The following day I told my new therapist of my dream and I associated to the words in a Bob Dylan song, "Blowin' In The Wind". I knew the answer to my life, the answer to my struggle, was blowing in the wind. The task of my life was how to don the leotards, to work through the psychological issues that blocked my embracing them; who I am in my inner core is most easily experienced and transmitted through the aesthetic and procedural knowledge expressed within my dance.

In hindsight, what was wonderful is that those leotards in my dream existed in my real life. There was hope; the dream signaled my "forward edge strivings" (Tolpin, 2002). I had bought a whole stash of the same leotard on sale. I have never subjected them to the heat of a dryer, but, with care, I only let them hang dry. Consequently, they have lasted through many years of sweat, toil and joy. Donning them is a deep pleasure. The basic premise of my dream, of my life, has never changed. My need to feel and to evolve developmentally who I am aesthetically, and in so doing to feel an empathic tie with myself and others, to participate in a co-constructed world of empathy, is ongoing.

Lachmann (2001) suggests we "consider psychoanalysis an art form like poetry and music . . . Analyst and analysand are both performers and listeners, co-composing an analytic interlude to celebrate the unique individuality we prize: our dissonant natures, our chromatic emotions, and our atonal self states" (p. 177). We emphasize that as part of that cross-modal aesthetic exchange, psychoanalysis, like all of life, is a dance, capturing the aesthetic and empathic foundation of our shared humanity.

Part II

George Hagman

In this section we would like to discuss the clinical implications of the understanding of the aesthetic sense of self and self-with-other that has been presented in the prior section. Most importantly we intend to illustrate through a clinical example the intersubjective, interactional nature of the aesthetic dimension of analysis and its role in the elaboration of empathy and the therapeutic process.

Jim, a man in his thirties with strong professional aspirations and a compulsion to accommodate others and neglect his own needs, would enter my office and after a thoughtful pause, as if collecting his thoughts, would begin again, taking off from what he remembered about our last session. He would discuss his frustration as a consultant, his inability to find ways to express his personal vision and creative ambitions. He would tell me of his relationship with his girlfriend. He described her as overly anxious, dependent and needy. His emotional life was focused continually on trying to calm her, if not make her happy – his needs were on hold. He even claimed to have lost touch with simple wishes of his own. He said he did not have any idea what he wanted.

In many ways Jim was an ideal patient and he handled the technicalities of our relationship well. He was reliable, arrived early and paid on time. Invariably verbal, he was thoughtful and self-analytical. However, I was aware from the start, that despite these positive qualities, something was off. It was more in the feel of being with him, the quality of our interactions, physically, the changing relative positions of our bodies, the mutual adjustments in tone, volume and timbre of voice, the shape of our dialogue, as our imagery and constructed narrative were woven as if on a loom of many gradually intertwining colored strands. But the mix was wrong, the weave awkward and off line, the dialogue clumsy, our voices clashing, off beat, and flat. Our aesthetic dance was out of sync.

All human relationships have aesthetic dimensions, whether this is the mutual fittedness of the mother holding and playing with her baby, a presentation to the board of directors of an advertising agency, or the physical engagement of analyst and patient. These interactions are shaped by formally encoded, procedural representations that are models for participation in later relationships. This implicit, procedural memory organization possesses a particular set of aesthetic dimensions which capture and create the "feel" of life, of self and of self-in-relation. The psychoanalytic situation offers us an opportunity to experience and reflect on these aesthetic dimensions in a secure, structured and to an extent, controlled environment. We would say that the psychoanalytic situation is replete with aesthetic qualities which are stimulated and intensified by the structured yet intimate nature of the relationship.

The following is a partial list of aesthetic dimensions expressed through varying components of the psychoanalytic relationship:

1. Verbal interchange: rhythm, tone, color, and shape.
2. Physical interaction: the sensation of our bodies dynamically linked – the clinical dance.
3. Fantasy co-construction: structuring of narrative forms.
4. Visual: shape, shadow, light, color, depth, simplicity and complexity of form.
5. The "feel" of being together.
6. The aesthetic of therapeutic insight – shock, disruption and repair.

What role do these aesthetic dimensions play in the analytic process, and most importantly in successful therapeutic change? First, let us note that it is increasingly recognized that no one factor results in therapeutic change. Interpretation, once seen as the purest, most directly mutative component of technique, is now viewed within the context of many factors: security, attachment style, and attunement to mention several. This aesthetic dimension plays a non-specific role in psychoanalysis. These "non-specific factors" are viewed as being in the background, qualities of the relationship and/or context that can facilitate analysis but may not be "active ingredients" of change. Most importantly we have learned that non-specific factors can be powerful contributors to the process.

Empathy is one of the most important of these non-specific factors, the experience of which, we believe, possesses aesthetic dimensions. We talk about empathy as if it were a type of thinking and perhaps fantasy in which we imagine our way into the experience of the patient. Kohut called this "vicarious introspection". Recently this process has been understood as a co-construction in which both patient and analyst through a mutual process of communication (conscious and unconscious) develop a shared understanding of the patient's (and often of the analyst's) experience (Aron and Harris, 1998). Typically this view of empathy privileges its verbal, affective and imaginative nature.

In other words empathy is an intersubjective phenomenon that involves every level of engagement between patient and analyst. An important dimension of the analytic interaction, which contributes to the crystallization and elaboration of empathy (e.g. the sense of the other's inner life), is the aesthetics of the analytic exchange and situation. The analyst feels his way into the patient's inner world not vicariously, but through intense and sustained engagement in an interaction that is experienced in terms of rhythms, tones, shapes, colors, sensations and other qualitative aspects of formal organization. From this point of view empathy is not a type of imaginative work, but a "feeling into" the experience of the other, through attunement to their bodies, voice, visual appearance, even perhaps smell and feel. As with all other relationships, especially early attachments, this engagement stimulates mutual affects, fantasies and meanings, which compose the intersubjective matrix of empathy.

In other words, over time, both parties in analysis begin to develop a sense of "being" together. This occurs primarily on a physical and affective level. Our bodies respond to each other and we begin to identify a familiar feel within our bodies of the other – this may involve sexual feelings in our skin and genitals, defensive tensions in the mouth, the tightness of fear in the chest, aggressive arousal manifest by a stiffening neck and shoulders, as well as less pronounced, implicit states of comfort or discomfort as the sessions progress. We also are linked affectively with a range of emotions being elicited from each other. Over time we begin to be familiar with certain forms and patterns of feeling and body sensations. These make up the aesthetic dance of the relationship; the primary means by which we experience connection, attunement, and empathy.

Central to this aesthetic is the experience of its quality and value. In other words when we experience the analytic relationship aesthetically we make a judgment about its quality. In another context we refer to this experience as a value affect when love, excitement, pleasure or anxiety is directly tied to a qualitative judgment about someone or something. Fundamentally, value affects are not moral, but aesthetic, not about goodness or badness but about beauty, or on the other hand ugliness – and all that lies in between. There is, of course, no objective way to judge the quality of empathy, but we know it when we see and feel it.

In summary, empathy possesses aesthetic dimensions in which the "feeling of being together" crystallizes through interaction and is shared by the couple. And although we might not always be able to give this experience words, we are aware of it, it is the feeling of being together. Without some sense of the aesthetic, we have no way to judge the human meanings of our verbal statements and exchanges.

Of course much of this aesthetic experience is implicit and not necessarily conscious. In fact as we have argued, aesthetics has its source in formal aspects of the parent–child relationship that predate words and perhaps even the capacity of the child to elaborate the experience consciously (the unthought known, or unformulated experience).

By definition, a dimension cannot exist in isolation, rather each plays a part which is inseparable from and cannot be conceived of without being referenced to the other dimensions (length to width, width to height and depth, as well as time, each to all the other). So when we know an object we experience it and understand it within a simultaneously significant, multi-dimensional field. Clinically this means that the words and meanings that are exchanged necessarily possess an aesthetic dimension which has form, extension, and other qualities; these determine the "existence" of the content of the session, the "being" of the analytic couple. So the aesthetic dimension is not an extra, a pleasant trait. It structures the experience of being together at the deepest and most decisive level.

Once the analyst becomes aware of this aesthetic dimension and begins to organize her experience of the aesthetics on a conscious level, she can move this recognition to the forefront of her experience of the interaction, and we believe this can heighten the visceral understand of the relationship and even reveal previously unknown aspects of the clinical exchange. In fact it is when the aesthetic dimension is linked to and elaborated along with other dimensions (verbal, affective, narrative) that these other dimensions can be more clearly and forcefully appreciated within the interactional field of the analysis.

I learned that Jim was raised in a depressed and rather cruel family. His father, an academic, was often angry and did not offer Jim any opportunity for a sustained and involved relationship. Most importantly the father did not protect Jim from the mother, who Jim described as depressed and extremely self-centered. Jim learned the hard way to walk gingerly around the mother who was easily perturbed. When her needs or wishes were not met, Jim recalls, she would accuse him of selfishness and even betrayal. These accusations were frequent and predictable. Jim learned to attune himself to his mother's moods and attitudes. He could sense when to keep his distance and when to approach her. In other words they engaged in a form of "aesthetic dance" characterized by a fragile relationship between attunement and disruption. Mostly (and most damaging to him) he learned to be preoccupied with any potential need of his mother, hoping to avoid or blunt the impact of her anger and blame. This obsessive focus on the needs of the other resulted in a disruption of Jim's self-experience, part of which involved a developmental failure in the elaboration of his aesthetic sense of self. Instead of being self-centered, he became increasingly mother-centered, until as an adult, he was no longer aware of it. Eventually his entire being and all his emotional energy became other-directed, extending his defenses beyond his mother, as he became increasingly concerned with trying to keep everyone in his life satisfied and happy.

For example, symptomatic of these derailments in self-development, in sessions, Jim was unable to articulate any personal desire, need, or wish, other than that which was directed at others. He struggled to account for any hobbies or interests; nor was he able to say where he wanted to go on vacation, or even if he did. He would sit across from me, his shoulders stooped, looking flustered, unable to describe to me any interest or priority that he could call his own. His aesthetic experience of his life was flat, colorless without vitality. In one session he told me:

> My girlfriend, Jill, and I are going on a vacation next week, to the islands. I am afraid that it won't be any good. I am sure it will be a wonderful place, but it's me. I am afraid that I will get that feeling again – like I am not sure it is right, not what is best for me. I don't know what that is but it makes it hard to choose, as if I choose what I want it won't be the right thing that I will have chosen incorrectly.
>
> But you also say you don't have a clear idea what you would *want* to choose.
>
> Right. It ends up being a matter of luck, but of course I expect to feel disappointment, not fulfillment.

Being unable to articulate what he wanted, he nonetheless felt that he had to choose the right thing. But his "feeling of being" in his life had low aesthetic value, and there was no way that he could judge what was right for him, or what he preferred. There was no way to know what choice to make – so he did nothing in regards to his personal needs or wishes – he remained radically non-committal, or rather unable to decide.

Around and around in his mind he reworked this impossible puzzle, longing to accomplish something satisfying in life, but unable to act – a type of aesthetic Hamlet – he would soliloquize in his sessions, drab and plain, unengaged and uninspired – not exactly depressed, but suppressed and uninspired. His experience of life was of a world without pizzazz or beauty, a plain, uninviting place. On the contrary, during these sessions I always felt restless, my legs ached and I shifted uncomfortably in my chair. I experienced no position as relaxing as I maneuvered myself in the chair. I worried that this would upset him, since I obviously was uncomfortable and physically unresponsive to him.

However, he had had times in his life when this aesthetic wasteland had opened up and revealed to him another way of being. He recalled that as a child he spent summers in Cape Cod. One particular summer (he is not sure which one) he felt unusually excited by the town and the ocean beach. He remembers wandering the town and the dunes, reveling in the sun and salty beach air. The old gray-shingled beach houses seemed particularly charming to him. He played and wandered – a happy, lively and playful young boy. The memories of that summer remained with him and were the source of both hope and despair. Hope that he was indeed capable of such feelings, and despair that he might not recover that sense of creativity and vitality.

Much more recently, he told me that he had been walking down a New York street on a sunny day. Lost in thought, feeling hopeless and at a loss as usual, he looked up at one of the nearby buildings, where a broadleaved tree stood against a red brick wall. At that moment the sun was shining on the wall, and above was a bright blue sky. Unexpectedly, shockingly, he experienced a surge of joy, fascination, and enthrallment. This familiar sight suddenly seemed transcendent. He felt alive, stirred by excitement at the beauty of the scene.

> I know I am capable of such a feeling, but I don't know how to hold onto it. I want to so bad. I want to feel about my life something like that moment, or the summer at the beach. But then afterward, I am back where I was unable to feel, unable to be able to feel any confidence about what I want, or even what I love.

Jim was recalling powerful moments of positive and enlivening aesthetic experiences, during which his engagement with the world became infused with the excitement of light, color, shape, rhythm, tone and sensation. The quality of these aesthetic experiences was thrilling. The beach and the sunny building were beautiful and even sublime, things of high quality and formal perfection. He felt stirred within his deepest self, and alive like he had never felt before, or since. Kuspit (2006) has written about "aesthetic shock" in which all our expectations and assumptions are thrown over and a new and dazzling world is revealed to us. We feel as if we are confronted by a pure and basic reality, but at the same time it is beautiful, infused with vitality and hope. Having had a taste of such an aesthetic experience, Jim hungered for more – but despaired.

One habit that Jim had, often when he seemed frustrated and physically rigid, was to expel air from his nostrils. I was always startled, my stomach contracting in disgust, a bit revolted by the gesture. I would worry that mucous would be scattered about my office, or soil his clothes. He didn't seem concerned – nor was there any sign of discharge. The air from his nose seemed dry, harsh and contentless. But this habit of his also felt as a piece with his entire body posture and gestural style. He would sit across from me, his shoulders high, his arms held in an angular fashion, stiff and awkward. But most importantly I felt there was no physical engagement between us. My motions did not seem to affect his – my nods went unrecognized, no response from him to my smiles or changes in my body posture. As noted earlier often I was all aches and pains, shifting in my seat as I tried to get comfortable. My posture was obviously based more on my internal body experience, than a response to him. If this was a therapeutic dance, we were badly off beat, out of sync, stepping on each other's toes.

Not surprisingly, my ability to express my aesthetic sense, my way of feeling into his experience and my "being" with him was awkward, incomplete and at times, the best word would be "ugly". My normal physicality and firm touch became uncoordinated and uncertain, tentative as I repeatedly experienced disruption and a sensation of being off balance.

Clinically this aesthetic experience with Jim was a crucial element in my effort to attune to his experience. I groped my way through our interactions. I did not fight the feelings of anxiety, the mismatched and awkward comments and missed opportunities. These feelings, however awkward, were important guides to my own self-reflection and my growing "feel for" Jim's style and the evolving nature of his personal aesthetic of self, and of self-with-other. Certainly the content of our dialogue was crucial as we explored the immediate experience of his relationship with his girlfriend and its link to his traumatic past. However, my participation in this dialogue was not determined by rational decision-making, linear logic and/or conscious thought, perhaps more important was my developing aesthetic feel for our relationship, and the changing nature of that aesthetic over time.

Recently Jim entered my office, stood in front of my chair, and announced: "Hello" and took his seat. He smiled slightly (a bit sheepish I thought) and as he stood there, he appeared more relaxed; his body more open and visible to me as if for the first time. I knew something had changed. I could feel my own body become more relaxed and less uncomfortable and achy. He said: "I think this is helping." He explained that although perhaps it was hard to see in any one session that he had begun to be more honest about his feelings and what he wanted, especially with his girlfriend. "I am much less concerned about keeping her happy. I still worry about it, but I am much more willing to say what I feel and deal with the consequences."

He said that he felt that this would lead to some conflict but in the end it would allow his girlfriend to both understand him better and have to deal with him. He admitted that this increased the anxiety he felt about it not working out, but that if the relationship was going to change and grow, it was the only thing to do. As he spoke he gestured with his hands in a way that was new (at least to me) as he talked about his relationship he would throw his arms out, point with his fingers and I imagined him manipulating the image of his relations with his girlfriend with his hands. He was clearly more willing to play with his language and include his body in the communication in a more flexible, expressive and responsive way.

There had been no dramatic "moments of meeting", or disruptions and repairs to point to as an explanation of the changes that occurred in our relationship. Most of our sessions seemed to be an awkward but stubborn effort to keep on going, on my part to find ways to be better fitted to Jim, on his part to feel less restricted and more expressive. Together we had to find a rhythm and style of attunement, so that rather than lurching awkwardly into his monologue, there might be some space for me and then for us as well. The improvisational aspect of our relationship became more attuned, trusting and open, as we threw away "old scripts", and let our interaction unfold without restriction.

Apart from these very positive statements, it was the feeling of our being together that was most striking to me. Our dialogue became more animated and rhythmical. Our bodies felt more engaged and responsive. The aesthetic tone of the interaction was richer, lively and more brightly toned, not the austere, grayish and drab aesthetic of earlier sessions. These qualities were also accompanied by excitement, even a little joy, at our success but also I think at the way our value affects augmented each other. As the clinical discussion became more animated and mutual, improvisational if you will, I became aware how each of us had a part in cultivating and elaborating these aesthetic feelings, as if we were co-creating a work of art.

For example, my personal aesthetic style is to be physically present; my motions are strong and emphatic. I can be verbally loud and I gesture with various parts of my body as I talk. Aware that my style can be imposing, perhaps intimidating to some patients, I find the typical restraint of the analytic stance helpful. In Jim's case, because I experienced our interactions as disruptive and coarse, I believed strongly that I had to restrain and monitor my aesthetic style in the sessions because of its potential negative impact on Jim – in other words I had to learn to follow his lead. I would begin the sessions sitting quietly, relaxing my body and mind, letting myself begin to respond to him as he sat across from me. As if following my partner in a dance, I would allow him to lead, offering myself as a responsive other, willing to attune myself to his voice, body movements and gestures – this was not easy for me but I continually righted myself, monitoring the feel of my responses and his reactions to them. Our awkwardness and uncertainty was obvious, our steps uncertain and his lead rough and uncomfortable, but I adjusted, absorbed this ugliness and made the most out of our rough dance. But more than that, I also followed him as he shaped and structured the dialogue, creating a narrative of our session, coauthors of a short story.

Another way to visualize this approach is to imagine the session as a type of Squiggle Game (Winnicott, 1971) writ large (in other words an improvisation) – he would act or talk, I would respond, he would take off from my remark, and we would gradually construct a form of being together – a form that had many facets, shapes, tones, lines, rhythms, colors and sensations. However, not simply an equal partner, I was also his analyst/instructor, reflecting back to him my observation of his manner of relating, probing his sense of self, and facilitating the structuring of his self-experience through interpretations. In other words I sought to articulate and attune the empathic link, to deepen formal organization of our being together, and of his sense of himself. When I say that this approach was like a dance, it was actually more like a dance lesson, or a corrective dance. But in this dance I was not just a partner and instructor but also student. I needed to learn his style, but also offer my own style in a responsive fashion, which would eventually crystallize into an aesthetic of our own, a signature style for our relationship.

As illustrated in this vignette from the analytic work with Jim, our aesthetic sense of self and of self-in-relation to others, as well as our capacity for empathy are intimately intertwined. Thus the aesthetic dimension of analytic therapy is not only a source of information but plays an important role in the therapeutic process. It also plays a role in the experience of each partner, and by increasing our awareness of and sensitivity to the vicissitudes of our aesthetic engagement with our patients we, as therapists, can engage in the therapeutic interaction at a richer and more fundamental level of communication.

We have argued in this chapter for a perspective on the analytic process based on awareness of this "aesthetic responsiveness". We have traced this process back to the nonverbal emotional rapport and empathy of the earliest infant-parent interplay when empathic bonds and our sense of aesthetic were an inherent part of the early relational interactions between parent and baby. We hope the reader will increased his or her awareness of and sensitivity to the aesthetic dimensions of the analytic relationship, thereby opening up a rich and complex realm of psychotherapeutic opportunity.

Chapter 5

Creative analysand

> It is the client more than the therapist who implements the change process. If the client does not absorb, utilize, and follow through on the facilitative efforts of the therapist, then nothing happens. Rather than argue over whether or not "therapy works" we could address ourselves to the question of whether or not the "client works"! In this regard, there needs to be reform in our thinking about the efficacy of psychotherapy. Clients are not inert objects upon whom techniques are administered. They are not dependent variables upon whom independent variables operate . . . It is important to rethink the terminology which assumes that "effects" are like Aristotelian impetus causality. As therapists have depended more upon the client's resources, more change seems to occur.
>
> (Bergin and Garfield, 1994, pp. 825–826)

Since Freud's initial formulation of the Basic Rule, which prescribed that the analysand surrender control and report whatever comes to mind, most psychoanalysts have viewed the analysand as a largely passive recipient of the analyst's therapeutic efforts (Schafer, 1967). Favoring inaction over intention and compliance over initiative, analysts came to view the analysand's active intention and creativity critically, as a type of symptom, or a sign of resistance, "acting out" or more recently, "enactment", but rarely as a healthy striving for growth and change. Even contemporary analytic thinkers, such as the relational analysts, de-emphasize the analysand's self-efficacy and autonomy as they focus on the social and interpersonal dimensions of psychological life. I contend that the model of the passive analysand has limited our understanding of the analytic process and in particular the analysand's contribution. We each have the motivation and capacity to creatively construct and reconstruct our self-experience and our relation to our world, and to make use of what's available to identify and pursue our goals and interests (Klein, 1976; Weiss, 1994, 1998; Slavin and Kriegman, 1998). One of the ways that people seek to do this is through psychoanalysis and the analytic relationship, "making use of" the resources offered by the analyst and the analytic method. This chapter discusses how analysands are creative in their own change process. In particular I will explore the role of the analyst and analytic treatment in facilitating and supporting the analysand's inherent motivation and creative capacity for self-reorganization and self-healing.

There has been much debate and substantial research devoted to determining the efficacy of psychoanalytic therapy as well as the psychotherapeutic mechanisms that the form of therapy may possess. We have found, similar to other forms of non-analytic therapy that analytic therapy is effective. However, we don't really know why. In addition given the general effectiveness of most forms of psychological therapy, we have not considered that the real agent of change may not be the therapy itself, but the participation of the patient. It may be that patients find a range of different types of therapy useful in making change, and analytic therapy may offer a particular type of assistance which some patients find useful.

I will argue in this chapter that the efficacy of any form of psychotherapy (analysis included) lies in the usefulness that it has for people as they make change within their selves and in their lives (Bohart and Tallman, 2003). In regards to standards of efficacy in psychoanalysis Owen Renik (2003) has argued that the judgment of excellence in analysis should rest on the patient's self-assessment – specifically the question as to whether the treatment has been of benefit to him or her. Our understanding of the analytic process frequently neglects this perspective – that is, analysands work hard in multiple areas of their lives, in session, at home, at work, within their own minds, to make sense of their experience, deal with problems and make change. Analysis is effective the extent to which the analysand finds the analyst and the treatment process useful in this effort. And while there are many ways that we can imagine analysis being useful to people, it is the *particular* way that an individual analysand makes use of their relationship with his or her analyst that matters. For example Weiss and Sampson (1986) have argued that analysands attempt to follow a specific plan to disprove certain negative expectations, and that it is the analyst's job to help him or her fulfill their goals for treatment. Given this, I believe that we can improve the effectiveness of analysis if we better understand the patient's self-healing processes, and the obstacles (both psychological, biological and social), which impede the analysand's efforts. That being said practicing analysts and analytic authors tend to focus one-sidedly and predominantly on the analyst's role in the treatment process, while the analysand is presented as generally passive. However even the best clinical strategies and techniques will fail if the analysand cannot make use of them, and it is when our approach supports the analysand's change efforts that we are most effective.

Some have argued that there is a conflict between the interests of the analyst and the analysand (Slavin and Kriegman, 1998). However I believe that frequently this conflict is exacerbated by the analyst's tendency to exaggerate his or her own participation in and degree of influence over the clinical process, and most importantly, over the analysand's motivation, capacity and initiative to reflect, decide and implement change. This "deception" (Slavin and Kriegman, 1998) results not just in a denial of the truth of the analytic relationship, but also skews the balance of influence so that inevitably the analysand must resist and challenge the analyst's deception if his or her interests are to be realized. Perhaps the one-sided emphasis on the analyst as the change agent is partially the result of the difficulties that analysts have with de-centering from their own experience and truly giving up the notion that he or she is in charge. Empathy is generally described as vicarious identification with the analysand's self-state and affective experience, not with the analysand's intentionality and initiative. We don't hear analyst's describing his or her sense of the analysand's experience of their own purposefulness and resourcefulness. These traits are usually viewed as absent or only present later in treatment after much of the therapeutic work is accomplished. It appears to be very hard for analysts to identify with the analysand's creative participation in the process, so the tendency is to focus principally on the analyst's role, leaving the analysand's part unarticulated and perhaps unacknowledged. In other words analysts appear to be generally more comfortable with the idea that they are the creative agent in the treatment, and they feel anxious at the thought of handing power over to the analysand (however illusory the analyst's power actually is). It is hard to accept that one is not in control, or that the method one is using is just one of many and its effectiveness based solely on whether the analysand finds it useful. So analysts tend to discuss their work as if there aren't various, often conflicting, approaches to analysis, all having legitimate claims to effectiveness. Or analysts exaggerate the efficacy of the analytic method, by the simple assertions regarding its clinical power. In the end analysts generally explain any curative effect as the outcome of their own interventions rather than the result of the analysand's own efforts and capacity for self-healing (the fact that it is usually the analyst who tells the story of the treatment and explains how it worked may also contribute to this imbalance).

Unfortunately I believe that this passive model impacts negatively on the analysand's self-experience, their view of the treatment relationship, and their understanding of the process of change. Many analysands identify with this passive self-image and experience themselves as submitting to the analyst's authority and expertise (there are strong societal supports for this attitude). Even if the treatment helps, the analysand often does not recognize their role in it, and the specific decisions and changes that he or she made to achieve her goals remains obscure. This may, in part, be due to the fact that the creativity of the analysand was not emphasized and never thoroughly explored during the analysis. I believe that if we place more emphasis on the analysand as problem solver and change agent, they will not only have a better understanding of themselves and how they accomplished change, but that the treatment process will be facilitated as the motivation and ability of the analysand to engage with the analyst in the process are recognized, supported and enhanced. As we find ways to make ourselves more useful, analysands will become more capable and effective in their own recovery process.

Dissociation, recognition and the analysand's use of the analyst

In action language, the person (or agent) performs actions, the meanings and goals of which are several or many and possibly unintegrated and paradoxical.

> Further, only some of these features may be realized consciously or preconsciously by the person, the remainder being enacted unconsciously.
> (Schaefer, 1983, p. 86)

Several decades ago Roy Schaefer (1976, 1983) proposed a new language for psychoanalysis in which he refuted the classical model that objectified subjectivity creating metapsychological constructs which denied the creative, intentional nature of psychological life. He argued that all mental experience (thinking, wishing, and every type of emotional creativity) was intentional, and could be reinterpreted and redescribed as "action". The problem is that many (if not most) actions may have different, sometimes paradoxical, meanings and therefore some activities are conflicted given the contradictory meanings by which they are viewed by the analysand. Hence, to say that the analysand is purposeful and in control does not mean that these processes are conscious, or that the intentions of the analysand are not conflicted. In fact one of the most common experiences of analysands is of themselves as victims, either of external events and/or people or of internal processes, which they feel they have not chosen and cannot control. Hence they come to analysis consciously seeking the ministrations of the professional healer, whose expertise and clinical armamentarium will hopefully cure them (Daphne Markin's recent article about her "Life in therapy" is a good example of this). The analysand constructs a view of himself or herself as passive so as to attempt to master the impact of the trauma. Unfortunately, the analyst, by holding to the passive model of the analysand, participates in the deception, or more precisely, enacts in the analytic relationship the dissociation which the analysand is using to cope with the potential internal conflict, and/or fear of retraumatization.

Many people, especially those who have endured trauma, dissociate the experience of their own creativity from the experience of helplessness associated with the trauma (Schafer calls this *disclaimed action*). This may primarily be an attempt to protect against the experience of shame, blame and/or guilt associated with the choices they made in the midst of trauma or the way in which they adapted in the aftermath of trauma. In all human situations choice and intentionality are present; however the recognition of many of the actions we have taken, especially those associated with survival, may feel unendurable. The ultimate acknowledgment of personal responsibility and creativity, which is a part of all adaptive strategies, is important if the analysand is to fully understand their experience of and response to trauma, and the choices, which he or she made to protect themselves physically, socially, and psychologically. In fact I believe that it is essential to the self-healing process that the person appreciates the choices he or she has made and the actions (both behavioral and psychological) that he or she engaged in in response to trauma. George Klein stressed the importance of this reversal when he wrote: "The functional importance of such (creative) repetition of experience is that it produces a form of control and integration; the self is able to make the experience happen. The basic aim is to 'own' the experience: its alien status and disconnectedness from the self are reduced by a self-governed re-experiencing of it" (Klein, 1976, p. 262). The recognition that you construct and manage your internal world, also means you can understand your intentions and change them, transforming your self-experience from victim to agent.

The creative analysand

Initially Heinz Kohut (1972) utilized a classical model of the passive analysand. This was due to both his reliance on a drive-based metapsychology and to a commitment to the traditional configuration of the analytic relationship as being the creative analyst treating the passive patient. The analyst viewed the evocation of archaic fantasies and desires for selfobject experiences as a byproduct of particular characteristics of the situation and of his or her skillful management of the treatment. Even the most important change process, transmuting internalization, was viewed as a non-directed, passive structuralization process, not an effort by the analysand to develop and acquire capacities and skills as a result of their participation in the therapeutic effort.

However, from another point of view, Kohut also began to change the way he viewed the analysand's creativity. He came to believe that it was his willingness to understand the patient's efforts at self-repair that forced him to question the highly passive and mechanistic views of traditional analytic practice. For example he eventually recognized that Mr Z was desperately trying to use Kohut to repair his self-damage and, at least in the first analysis, he was unsupported and gave up. Only when Kohut saw what the analysand was trying to do and then got out of the way of the process, was Mr Z then able to make full use of the analysis. In this case Kohut's empathy was not just about Mr Z's self-state or affects, but a detailed inquiry into how Mr Z was attempting to use his analyis for self-repair as he completed his previously derailed developmental tasks.

Unfortunately there are some aspects of Kohut's theory that maintain the passive model. For example he generally viewed the expression of the selfobject transferences in treatment as evoked or emergent, rather than as psychological activities of the analysand. It is as if the analysand has no part in the development and expression of these fantasies about the analytic relationship. However, I believe that it is much more useful to see selfobject experiences as attempts by the analysand to engage in modes of relating which are highly useful to self-repair and self-efficacy. Recently, Marian Tolpin addressed several issues similar to the idea of the creative analysand that we are discussing here.

In her chapter "Compensatory structures: Paths toward the restoration of the self" (1997) Tolpin argued that the tendency of psychoanalysts to limit their understanding of transferences to the archaic, childhood sources, has resulted in a misunderstanding of later developmental needs as well as the healthy, normal motivation of most people to seek out and make use of relationships that can repair and/or enhance vulnerable areas of the self. Her discussion of the selfobject transference involves a depiction of the patient as an agent of change as he or she seeks to recover from trauma, by turning away psychologically from developmentally thwarting relationships, and seeking new experiences that can compensate for self-deficits.

In Tolpin's later important chapter "Doing psychoanalysis of normal development: Forward edge transferences" (Tolpin, 2002) she expanded on this idea:

> The deepest layer of the psyche consists of strivings of the forward edge – once normal needs of the unmirrored self, of the self that is chronically enfeebled and/or fragmenting and is in search of idealized strengths, of expanding alikeness experiences with a kindred soul. It is the reactivation of these needs in selfobject transferences that is potentially transforming – the needs and the therapists' responses to them can revitalize the self, restore the urge to complete development, and get development back on track.
>
> (p. 183)

Despite the objectified and passive language, the implications for a new understanding of the analysand's creativity are obvious in terms like "striving", "search" and "urge". In her discussion of the patient Matt (as discussed by Egan and Kernberg, 1984), Tolpin described a young man and his search for a new relationship to help him break free from a lifetime of self-denigration and to engage in a process that will help him continue his thwarted developmental journey. Later in the chapter, after the analyst has repaired earlier failures and established with Matt an adequate mirroring selfobject transference, Tolpin notes:

> Matt was no longer so entirely alone and lonely in his splendid isolation – his treatment established a self-selfobject transference that reinstated phase-expectable encouragement, mirroring and guidance. The analyst was a "usable selfobject" if you will and Matt was enabled to make use of his multiple development-enhancing functions, including his function of interpretation.
>
> (Tolpin, p. 184)

For Tolpin, at the "forward edge" of any transferences the analyst can identify the patient's healthy attempts to solve problems, seek out new opportunities and bring about changes that can create new relationships and restore a damaged sense of self. She believes that analysts must try to identify these healthy activities that she believes are present often in the most negative transferences and interpret them, support them and collaborate with the patient as he or she seeks to change – in other words, to offer him or herself as a "usable selfobject".

In sum, Tolpin wrote that the role of the analyst was to provide the context in which opportunities for selfobject experiences are made available and in which the patient feels able to safely express selfobject needs and expectations. From this perspective, analysands are not just passive recipients of developmentally needed responses, but creative people, striving to find satisfaction and opportunities to actualize their ambitions and interests. The creativity of the analyst is to attend to and support this relational context, interpret any anxieties related to the experience and expression of personal activities and interests; and finally to identify and support the client's efforts to renew development and to accomplish the psychological and relational ambitions that are important to him or herself.

Traditionally, we talk about the selfobject experience as serving a "function" for people. This reflects the view that a person is the recipient of this function. I suggest that we take a different view. Rather than serving "functions" I would argue that selfobject experiences are psychologically "useful" to the analysand. In other words, the key characteristic of selfobject experience is the way the person uses the psychological experience of the analyst to make change. In addition, selfobject experience is not *evoked* – rather the analysand and analyst work together to create the conditions for the analysand to organize new ways to experience us and a more powerful way of making use of the therapy. Hence, expanding on Tolpin's work, I would argue that there is always a "forward edge" to all transferences, even the most negatively organized ones. The job of the analyst is to help the analysand see that "edge", work with it and help them build on it. If we are successful the patient will find us to be "usable selfobjects" and he or she will make use of the functions we make available to resume work on previously derailed developmental challenges.

The analysand's activities

Analysands decide to enter analysis because earlier strategies that they have attempted to reduce their distress and make change, have not worked. Usually they view themselves as powerless and they keep repeating, often obsessively, an increasingly limited, frustrating, and ineffective set of behaviors, feelings and relationships. They complain that they do not feel in control of their lives and they are hoping that the analyst can do something about it. (See Daphne Merkin (2010) for a description of the author's lifelong search for a powerful analyst who could "fix" what was wrong with her.)

The analysand's decision to enter analysis is an indication of the forward edge, a hopeful tendril of decisiveness and action that may be built upon. In the midst of all the suffering, complaining and despair, it is important to identify how the analysand is hoping to use the analysis to "get better". In fact even when the initial transference responses are negative or hostile, it is important to recognize how that negativity may also reflect healthy striving. Analysands often seek both to protect and defend what they experience as their vulnerable selves, while at the same time risking being open to another person, to change, and they fear, perhaps, retraumatization. In addition, most transferences are not completely rigid and unchanging, many clients despite their apprehensions will willingly modify and adapt their expectations if given a chance. So the assumption here is that all people have remnants of health and in some, perhaps hidden, way they creatively seek to engage in relationships and alter themselves, so that they can continue development, feel happier and find more satisfying relationships.

That being said, analysands engage their analysts at the beginning of treatment in familiar, defensively organized ways. Understandably they feel vulnerable and uncertain about their options. There is no reason to trust the analyst, so they don't. Yet at the same time the analysand tries to hold onto hope and wants to trust the analyst, perhaps desperately so, but such longings also involve tremendous psychological risk. Thus the analysand organizes the relationship and manages the interaction to simultaneously assure self-protection and also to create openings to change. From this perspective, transference based on the current application of past relational models is an effort to test the therapist in order to check if he or she is truly a new person, or just the same old traumatogenic object (see Weiss and Sampson, 1986).

Unfortunately the resulting balance between protection and hope may lead to an experience of paralysis. To accomplish change means to become vulnerable to dreaded retraumatization, hence you resist change. And this goes round and round, often getting the patient nowhere. However it is also true that the analysand strives, despite this dilemma, to engage the analyst and make use of what he or she has to offer. The urge to move forward, to risk change, hangs suspended in the dilemma. In order to change, the analysand has to find (or risk) a new way of using the analyst. One way is through selfobject experience, but the analysand's willingness to engage the analyst in this healing transference depends on the analyst's reponse.

The selfobject transference is a modality of relating that is fundamental to human relatedness. When we experience another as a selfobject we grant them an importance and degree of power that other relationships do not have. By idealizing the other we invest the relationship with an extraordinary usefulness. At the same time, we also feel indebted to and invested in the other in ways that feel enormously risky. "If I depend on you so much, if I come to rely on you in these important ways, you may let me down, reject me, shame me. Just as others have done in the past."

So during the initial phase of analysis (what Kohut calls the "understanding" phase) the analysand may be reluctant to idealize the analyst and may not make much use of him or her. The analyst tactfully describes the analysand's dilemma, carefully identifying the search that brought the person in, and the ways in which the analysand is trying to both protect and change the self. Over time the analyst interprets the analysand's fears of idealization and dependency. Most importantly the anxiety about how the analysand's internal self-organization may be disrupted as he or she experiences longings toward the increasingly important analyst, and finally risks making use of the analyst.

Eventually, the analysand may begin to idealize and try to make use of the analyst in this new way. This is often a precarious situation and the anxiety about failure can be strong. The analysand is acutely sensitive to any indication that the analyst is not supportive, not empathic, or otherwise incapable, unwilling or negatively motivated – this may involve a period of testing the analyst with the hope of disproving negative expectations and fears. The analysand withdraws trust and then reinvests the analyst; often in response to the clinical interventions that the analyst makes use of in an attempt to respond to the analysand's needs and fears.

With time and in the absence of any experience of renewed trauma, most analysands begin to organize their experience of the analyst in some form of stable configuration of selfobject fantasies and modes of relating. This sustained selfobject transference can be very useful to the analysand as they work to improve their self-esteem, effectiveness, and the types of relationships they engage in. However, this way of using the analyst may depend on the maintenance of an illusion that the analyst is perfect, exquisitely attuned and powerful, or that the analyst is admiring, encouraging or incredibly confident in the analysand. Or that the analysand and analyst share such a wonderful relationship that they are capable of any challenge when together. These illusions are only useful for a time, and must be given up. Inevitably, the analysand describes the analyst as failing him or her, and thus not as reliable and empowering as was once thought; so new ways to make use of the analyst need to be developed.

Recognizing that the analyst is also an independent person (not under the patient's control) and not as powerful and ideal as he or she thought, the analysand begins to separate fantasy from reality. On the other hand, if the analysand's use of the analyst as a selfobject (transference) is prematurely and/or traumatically disrupted before the analysand has adequately integrated the experience and has not as yet gained confidence in change then the analysand may doubt the therapist, become threatened and anxious, lose confidence, and re-engage in strategies to protect themselves from additional loss and greater trauma.

In the following case report I will discuss my work with a patient who initially described his problems as outside his control and not connected with any creativity or intention on his part. I will show how the initial phase of the analysis involved an exploration of the function of this disclaimed action and the importance of exploring how his apparent victimization was, in fact, an adaptive response to family trauma. Repeated interpretations of his response to loss led to increasing insight into his survival strategy and a more positive approach in dealing with current life problems and attitudes toward himself.

Case example: Pat

Pat, a 32-year-old male lawyer, sought psychoanalytic psychotherapy because of persistent feelings of hopelessness and preoccupations with fantasies about personal loss and professional failure. He described how he ruminated throughout the day (almost all his waking hours) about possible scenarios where he would make a mistake on his job or encounter a problem with his boss, and the result would be calamity. This dread of looming disasters had gradually increased over the past five years and had recently become so intrusive and unbearable that he sought help. Initially Pat was dismissive and negative about the possibility of help. "There's no point. The reality is that if I fuck up it will be a disaster. The only problem is I just can't stop thinking about it, and there is no way to stop it. No matter what I try to do. It's like a black cloud hanging over me all the time."

When Pat was 18 years old his mother was diagnosed with cancer. His father, an odd and withdrawn person, was distant and unemotional with Pat and his brother about her illness and death. Pat does not remember having any emotional reaction. "I felt nothing . . . at least nothing that I can remember." Soon after her death he went away to college. "I just continued what I was supposed to do. I had planned to be a lawyer, so I studied the law. I think I hated it, but I really never questioned the decision. That was just what I did."

Over the next few years Pat constructed a set of beliefs centering on the dangers of the world. "It didn't begin right away. I graduated and got my first job. I began to notice certain fears, and then they just got worse. Until now, they're overwhelming. I don't know why I am even here. There's not much you can do about it."

Pat experienced his anxiety as something that happened to him, as an accurate depiction of the world and an irrevocable part of his reality. However, I began to point out to him the protective function of these beliefs. They were warnings to himself, self-protective beliefs, and as long as he stayed on his guard he would be ready for any disaster that came along. I noted the impact of maintaining these beliefs on his willingness to make use of me. "If you ever allow yourself to trust me, to maybe consider that I might help you with these fears. Well then that would be a real danger. If you let down your guard here, then disaster will follow and you may not be prepared to deal with unexpected threats."

In response to the catastrophe of his mother's death and his father's withdrawal, Pat had constructed a set of beliefs that functioned as an "early warning system" for potential traumas that lurked around each corner (Bromberg, 1998). Part of his belief system involved a view of himself as a victim of circumstances, not as an actor forming his fate. He also organized his transference to protect himself from any feelings of dependency and need. If he trusted me he would open himself up to retraumatization and further loss. So he used me in a paradoxical fashion, making himself available to the therapeutic process and at the same time decrying my uselessness. Therefore he could make use of me, but at the same time he didn't have to risk the disruption of his "disaster preparedness" plan.

As I repeatedly interpreted his fear of and efforts to make use of me (and his self-protectiveness) I suggested to him the affective reactions and self-states resulting from the losses that he may have endured in his adolescence, and why he might experience them as unbearable. My goal was to inquire into and establish a dialogue about his apparent attitudes of fearfulness as an adaptive response to thwarted coping strategies, unbearable affects and experiences of profound uncertainty and isolation. All of his fears made sense if we understood them as strategies to survive and manage life without his mother. As a result his admitting that he might feel like he needed me, and desired some positive involvement with me, was threatening and he had to refute the potential benefit of therapy to insure that he remain on his guard and prepared for the worst, no matter at what cost.

In sum, in response to the collapse of his childhood world, Pat had constructed a system of beliefs that he could use to anticipate and protect against danger. He maintained this system for several years, but eventually found that the fearfulness and continual state of vigilance was becoming a problem in itself. Finally, just prior to entering treatment, he realized that his efforts to use his neurosis as an early warning system were turning out to be ineffective. Therapy was a new threat, so he had to find a way to put himself in a situation to use my help while simultaneously asserting the impossibility of change. With time, as a result of his experience of my empathy and the usefulness to him of my interpretations of the strategies he implemented to make sense of and cope with his traumas and losses, Pat began to change his approach to relationships at work as well as how he managed his depressive symptoms. No longer a victim he came up with effective strategies to manage his boss and decided to go on an antidepressant to better manage his anxiety and sleeplessness.

Summary

The traditional view of the analysand as a passive participant in the analytic process and the analyst as the creative change agent has been central to our understanding of psychoanalytic practice. However, this view denies the importance of the analysand as creative in treatment and may in fact confound and confirm the analysand's unconscious denial of their own intentionality. This chapter argues that the effectiveness of analytic treatment can be greatly enhanced if we adopt an approach that emphasizes and strengthens the analysand's potential to make more effective use of the analyst. This requires that we eschew passive terminology and address the forward edge, dimensions of the analysand's communications and behaviors.

From the perspective of the Creative Analysand, selfobject transferences are important ways in which people make use of their analysts. They experience us as: (1) enormously valuable and important to them, e.g. idealization; (2) as part of them, making use of us psychologically to make changes in self-image, affects, feelings of vitality, etc.; and as hopefully (3) durable and capable of surviving the stresses of analysis, and remaining useful throughout the change process. A case illustration is offered that highlights this viewpoint in analytic work with an adult analysand who lost his mother in adolescence.

Chapter 6

Creative analyst

> The creative worker, whether artist or scientist, reorganizes the world in some fresh way – the artist through developing forms, the scientist through new concepts. One mode – be it artistic form or scientific concept – is not more arbitrary than the other
>
> (Rose, 1980, p. 79)

As we have seen, psychoanalysts have always been interested in the creative process. Many, especially in the schools of object relations and self-psychology, have viewed creativity as a core human capacity – a prime criterion of mental health and maturity. Efforts have been made to identify the nature of the creative process but, for many, the idea remains appealing but ambiguous. This chapter discusses the dynamics of the analyst's creativity. I argue that the creative process is characterized by specific forms of feeling, thinking and, most importantly, relating that lead to the emergence of something new – therapeutic change. While the artist works with form and the scientist with concepts, the analyst works in the medium of the intersubjective field, the infinitely ambiguous constellation of human meanings that makes up the analytic relationship.

Several years ago I published an article on the artistic creative process (Hagman, 2000, 2006) where I proposed a self-psychological model that linked self-experience with the dialectic between inner and outer forms of subjectivity. In this chapter I show how the model of artistic creativity may be useful in understanding the analyst's creative process. I hope to accomplish several things: (1) to illuminate the many similarities between art and psychoanalysis; (2) to discover the differences and thus highlight the special creative elements in analysis; (3) to emphasis the creative features of ordinary analytic practice; and (4) to enhance the creativity of analytic work by cross-fertilizing our profession with the creative arts.

In any successful treatment the analyst and patient engage in a co-creative process that is characterized by innumerable interactions and interventions. Creativity is not found only in the exceptional moments; rather it is active throughout treatment. In most analysis, even those without dramatic developments, the creative process is at the heart of the day-to-day vicissitudes of the relationship itself. In particular I will show that creativity is found in the analyst's struggle to preserve, enhance and restore self-experience, specifically the sense of the *analytic self* as it emerges during the treatment process. This may seem like a strange assertion given our focus in the last chapter on the creativity of our patients, as well as our aim to facilitate change in the patient's psychological state. Despite the fact that most analysts feel satisfaction at the reduction of their patient's suffering, it is the skilled and effective practicing of the analytic craft that is one of our main sources of satisfaction. As with any profession the core motivation must be the confirmation of the experience of our professional self – which is enhanced proportionally to our success in understanding and helping our patients. Thus the paradox is resolved: we feel confirmed as analysts when we feel effective in understanding and helping our patients. But altruism is only a part of it, a primary motive is linked to self-experience, specifically our sense of our analytic self as it is actualized and is effected by the intersubjective field of the analytic relationship.

Most people identify creativity as the ability to do or make something new, or to invest something with a new appearance or form. In art the usual definition involves the use of imagination and skill. However many new things are of poor quality, poorly fitted, or counter to the welfare of the creator or others. Therefore to just do something new or different is not necessarily to be creative – it may even be simply a sign of impulsivity or even desperation. True creativity (especially in psychoanalysis) is not just different and new. Creativity in psychoanalysis must meet the following conditions: (1) it must involve a challenge to or an actual change in the psychological structures and/or processes for one or both members of the dyad, (2) it must encourage or compel development within the self-organizations of the patient and analyst, (3) it must be useful to the patient, or at least move the process towards the treatment goals, and (4) it must expand the nature of theory and practice, or elaborate them in a fresh way (not business as usual nor simply a provocation). It is important to note that these qualities might not be apparent initially (in fact some interventions may at first appear as mistakes or aberrations), but they must ultimately be recognized as clinically sound for us to credit the analyst with creativity (or the patient for that matter).

The above definition describes the conditions that must be met to call something creative, but it says little about the creative process in analysis, the subject of this chapter. To this end let me begin with a preparatory discussion of the notion of the analytic self. This is important to be clear about since as I noted above it is in the elaboration and perfection of the analytic self that is at the heart of the psychoanalyst's creativity.

The analytic self

In recent years a number of theorists have argued that self-experience, rather than being a unitary phenomenon, is complex and multiple. In other words, our sense of self involves a number of generally discrete sub-organizations that are activated in response to the demands of particular contexts and expectations. The ideal of the unitary self, the center of initiative, known for its cohesion and continuity has been the traditional model for healthy self-experience; however, recent approaches have stressed the mature capacity to permit a fluid and dynamic self-experience in which changing organizations of self experience are accepted and even cultivated. Rather than advocating a mono-organizational model of the self, we must acknowledge the advantages of containing many self-organizations within an overarching, coordinated, meta-self. In this regard, of central interest to us in this chapter are the vicissitudes of the Analytic Self, that is the self-organization of the professional analyst that is experienced by the analyst in the treatment situation.

In addition, the sense of self (in our case the *analytic self*) is not a fixed, unchanging structure but crystallizes out of and is embedded within relationships. In other words, our self-experience is highly contingent on our engagement with others, communications, physical transactions and modes of relatedness. Thus our sense of self depends on the mirroring of others, or maybe more precisely on a type of intersubjective system of meanings which is constructed out of the relational fields in which we live. The specific instance of the Analytic Self is a high-level self-organization that requires mature selfobject experiences to maintain, confirm and enhance it. These selfobject experiences may come from a variety of sources: colleagues, mentors, and students are several examples. But a primary source of selfobject experience is the activity of the analytic process itself, most importantly the relationship with the patient. We look to the treatment process to validate and nurture our sense of ourselves as analysts. At the same time, the analytic process is not just a series of events but a flow of interactions in which each actions follows from an other and then leads into another. The analytic self is an evolving, responsive structure. The flow of the analytic self both effects and responds to the changes occurring in the patient's and analyst's subjective worlds in interaction.

The organization of the analytic self is composed of numerous elements. No analyst, even the most "orthodox", is clear and uniform about her self-experience. The modern analyst as a result of the varieties of analytic theories and modes of practice must contain within her self numerous points of view, sets of values and representations of acceptable, optimal and ideal practice. The creative analyst allows for a diversity of analytic selves and cultivates the innumerable facets that each self must contain. Creative response often involves playing with various permutations of the analytic self, and the analyst ideally feels comfortable with this variety and can "stand in the spaces" (or perhaps more dynamically, "dance" in the spaces) of this multiplicity of analytic self-organizations (Bromberg, 1998).

We all like to see our patients get better, but if we come to depend on these positive experiences, it is a problem. An experienced and competent analyst must be able to find self-confirmation in all of the events, demands and even problems that make up the analytic relationship. In fact, I would argue that the creative analyst values those parts of the treatment process that are most challenging, even disturbing, for it is in those areas that solid professional and personal growth is grounded.

The creative process

Alan Roland, in his book "Dreams and Drama", referred to the organization of aesthetic talents, ambitions and identifications as the "Artistic Self". Roland discussed how artists seek to actualize this sub-system of the self through creative work (Roland, 2002, pp. 30–33). The artistic self is embodied in aesthetic form through the manipulation of a medium. However, the psychoanalyst seeks the actualization of their Analytic Self in the analytic/therapeutic process, which is brought about by means of and within the treatment relationship. This process is not abstract and de-personalized; rather it has the form and content of the personal professional sensibility of the analyst in a unique relationship to a given patient. The art of analysis is not an object, but an evolving conception of the treatment relationship – or to use Thomas Ogden's (1994) and Jessica Benjamin's (2004) terms "The Analytic Third" which is an intersubjective construction of analyst and patient in interaction. But what is important to us here is the way in which the analyst assesses and effects the meaning of the Analytic Self within that "Third".

The underlying desire of the artist is the externalization and idealization of subjective experience through the creation and refinement of aesthetic form. The desire of the analyst is to enact/externalize through the treatment process a form of the analytic self and by means of clinical management of the relationship to bring about an experience of the self as an analyst of quality, even perfection. In other words there is a wish in all of us to be good therapists and we work hard to achieve this in our work with patients. It is crucial to my thesis that this desire is difficult to achieve (especially when it is not an illusion), and even harder to maintain, but it remains our goal.

There may be some analysts who are not creative. They may follow a certain routine, nurture positive transferences and be dependent on good outcomes. Many patients benefit from such an approach but this is not the analyst we are discussing here. The creative analyst is continually motivated to engage in resolving the dialectic between the inner self and the externalized self within the transference/countertransference field. He or she seeks new forms of understanding, new organizations of meanings, new configurations of self and self-with-other.

An excellent example of the ordeal of the creative analyst is Heinz Kohut's account of his discovery of the selfobject transference. In those early years Kohut, ("Mister Psychoanalysis" as he referred to himself), was a practitioner of ego psychology, the dominant orthodox analytic model of that day. As a leader of organizational psychoanalysis he idealized the dominant clinical approach and values, and attempted to practice them faithfully. He wrote: "I mostly did what my colleagues did, and still do." However, he eventually found himself listening to the particular needs of his patients and an important tension developed between his theoretical allegiances and what he believed to be the narcissistic needs of his patients. For a time he tried to avoid the rising conflict within his analytic self by devoting himself to administrative work (1984, p. 87–88). But over time Kohut's ability to sustain his sense of his analytic self was challenged. He found that his treatment approach had to change (as well as his theory) in order to bring his engagement with the patient into line with his new observations and developing beliefs. Once he was able to move beyond his old self-organization (to escape from the inner conflicts resulting from his new beliefs) and respond creatively to his patient, he began to articulate and actualize an entirely original self psychology and treatment method. It was this creative dialectic between an old organization of his analytic self and the new emergent self-organization based on the selfobject tie with his patient, that a fresh approach crystallized.

Kohut's insights into the centrality of the psychology of the self occurred in response to his treatment relationship with Mr. Z. It was not just a "scientific finding" devoid of passion and struggle. What Kohut described was a period of self-disorder, held at bay for a time by his focus on non-clinical work, but nonetheless it was an experience of crisis in the organization of his analytic self. Old idealizations had to be abandoned and a new way of being an analyst had to be acknowledged and actualized. Although in his account he emphasized the theoretical dimension, the transformation was also profoundly personal, involving dialectic between the empathic self of the transference and the classical self of his professional allegiance. The resolution of this tension resulted not just in a change in Kohut's analytic self, but to a revolution in the self-experience of a significant segment of the analytic profession.

The creative dialectic

The creative artist is always interested in what is new and unexpected in his or her work. But the new is not simply found; it is created/produced through a dialectic tension between the self-experience (feeling) and the externalized subjectivity of the artist as manifest in the artwork. It is this need to reconcile the inner and outer aspects of self-experience that drives the creative process forward.

> From the first moment of creation the artist engages in dialectic with the selfobject/artwork. The artist extend his subjectivity outward and alters the medium. From this point on there is something new, which has been created out of a merger between the self-experience of the artist and the object world. The work in progress exists. The artist continues to observe the work, appraises it, and there is a dialectic between that which has been created and the subjectivity and judgment of the artist. The dialectic is between two realms of self-experience, that which is internal/subjective and that which is external/objective. Each influences the other (the imaginary and the manifest) and the result is further creation.
>
> (Hagman, 2000, p. 287)

The creative artist does not just change an object, altering its appearance to match some internal image of the potential artwork (although this non-creative approach to art is all too common); he actively extends his imagination to the object, which becomes both object as well as an objectification of the artist's subjectivity. Through further creative activities the artist refines the subjective object, thus moving the artwork towards higher level of aesthetic organization and expressive perfection.

The analyst's work within the transference-countertransference field is similar to the artistic process described above. Analytic creativity also emerges from a dialectic tension as the analyst engages with aspects of her analytic self-transformed by the patient's subjectivity – trying to perfect that which is at once part of them, but in fact no longer truly theirs. In this our motives are not simply concern for the patient's welfare, but the fate of our own subjectivity and self-experience, as it is subject to the vicissitudes of the clinical process. How does this work?

There is no initial point in this dialectic; so to discuss it we have to break into the treatment process at a particular point. Let's start with the patient who has a need/wish to fulfill certain fantasies related to selfobject needs, but due to fears of rejection or failure, a set of defensive maneuvers are also mobilized to protect self-experience during the dialogue with the analyst (the repetitive dimension of the transference is in the foreground, the selfobject in the background). The patient externalizes these needs and defenses through specific communications and enactments that are received by the analyst who internalizes them and reconciles them with his or her unique professional sensibility. In this way an aspect of the patient's subjectivity is now part of the analytic's subjective world. From this perspective the boundaries between the analytic self and the patient's self are fluid and the two realms are dynamically engaged across a porous psychological frontier. The patient now confronts aspects of him or herself within the analyst, and further activities will involve responses to this externalized self. The analyst, having taken in aspects of the patient, and reconciled them to her own subjectivity, attempts to actualize the analytic self through formulations and interventions. Most commonly the analyst interprets. The interpretation is an aspect of the analyst's subjective world (an amalgam of self and patient subjectivity) that is now taken in by the patient, who is affected by it (either defensively or progressively). Thus the analyst now engages a changed (for better or worse) patient and the subjective elements of the analytic self (the internalized interpretations). Thus the series of ongoing analytic interpretations include both the patient's self-state and the aspects of the analyst's subjectivity that have become part of that field (the transference). Creative developments emerge from this dialectic: the analytic self (countertransference) acts on the patient's self (response to the analyst's interpretations), resulting in a new emergent organization. This cycle unfolds in an ongoing process and will only end when the treatment is terminated (and may continue even after that point in a modified form within the mind of the patient).

Phase 1: Preparation, inspiration and self-crisis

The artist begins to formulate an intention (generally a feeling, idea or image that will make up the nucleus of the creative work). With this he or she identifies and prepares the required materials, and a context is set up within which the work will be done. Often artists have very specific requirements for their studio, the condition of their tools and even the time of day. In addition there are feelings, fantasies and needs that characterize the artist's psychological state. In other words, the artist sets up the conditions, contexts and prerequisites for work. These rituals can be understood as holding environments or containers that provide a background of safety so that the artist can engage in the risky business of creation.

> During this phase the artist tries to access every aspects of conscious and unconscious subjectivity. Doubt, uncertainty, and confusion may trouble the artist, alternating with joy and exhilaration the artist accesses each mark on the canvas and responds with an internal adjustment of fantasy. He experiences a heightening of attention, characterized by tension and often discomfort, which leads to a deepening responsiveness to the work.
>
> (Hagman, 2000, p. 286)

Like the artist, the analyst prepares herself for creative work. Coming into the office from her outside life, and entering the office, she begins to settle into a state of mind and readiness to assume the role of analyst. The office is arranged in a certain fashion, the chairs are positioned, and the appointment book and reading glasses set carefully on the table near the chair. She may consult some past notes, read some letters, make a couple of phone calls, all part of preparing the analytic self for there first patients. As the day unfolds the analyst moves from patient to patient and, with each encounter, different aspects of the analytic self emerge, and are elaborated in different ways. There is an evolving responsiveness to analytic work. In this context, as the sense of each impending role crystallizes in the analyst's mind and body, a good deal of conscious and unconscious preparation is engaged in. The analytic self begins to be organized anew and readied for work with each patient – these personal rituals may play an important role in the maintenance of the analytic self. It is however important to note that the degree to which this professional self is organized at any particular time is variable. Some analysts experience a very clear and firm sense of their analytic self; others have a more ambiguous and variable self-experience. I would argue that optimally the analytic self should not too rigidly set, that the analyst should feel this self as a potential, but also allow for a flexibility and multiplicity that will allow for a secure sense of self combined with the readiness for responsiveness that characterizes the best creative work.

Wilfred Bion (1961) said that there should be two anxious people at the start of an analytic session: the patient and their analyst. In fact, the creative analyst must be open to the experience of anxiety, and perhaps even welcome it, as she seeks to be responsive to the patient's unique self-organization and mode of relating. Often there are periods of "unknowing" and disorganization during which the analyst may feel confused, uncertain and doubtful about the integrity of her analytic self. Creative work is an effort to resolve this disorganized and anxious condition through the medium of the analytic treatment. In fact, I would argue that to be creative an analyst (similar to the artist) must cultivate anxiety, acknowledge the feeling, reflect on its meanings and sources, and have the courage to not close down the experience too quickly. Self-crisis is essential to most forms of creativity and likewise the creative analyst must welcome the disruption of the analytic self so that new forms of self-organization can emerge within a changing intersubjective field.

The artist has canvas, stone, or orchestra, the analyst's medium is the transference-counter transference field, an interpersonal zone in which reality and illusion coexist and interpenetrate each other. The artist has a brush chisel or pen, the analyst has interpretations, the words or actions that convey meaning to the patient, and contribute to or perturb the relational field. The patient is not a blank canvas, passive and blankly ready for the analyst's touch, rather the patient is like an actor, a dynamic rich subjectivity in and of herself, making psychoanalysis a shared process. Thus the analyst is not molding pliant clay but engaging in a dialogue in which the boundaries between self and other are simultaneously clear and permeable. The analyst's interpretations are also products of dialogue (although they are enriched by the analyst's store of theory and experience) and they are highly relevant to the patient's experience, but they are also fundamentally products of the analytic self in interaction, and thus they can be said to embody the subjectivity of the analyst. Interpretations are offered and assumed by the patient into her subjective world, thus the subjectivity of the analytic self can be said to come to exist as a part of the other/patient, who is, to an extent, changed by them. However, these changes are not necessarily creative, in fact commonly the patient reorganizes the analytic self into the invariant organizing principles – thus making their fate an object of further analysis.

Henry, a 16-year-old schizophrenic man (bright and creative despite his illness), would march into my office, and throw himself down into the chair with one leg cast over the arm rest. He would rarely initiate talk and seemed always to be impatient, as if this was the last place he wanted to be.

> I would often tremble with uncertainty and worry. My sense of myself as an analyst would be totally wiped out as I just tried to get through the session, just to make a little sense of what was going on.
>
> I interpreted and questioned in a vain effort to connect to him: "It must be hard to trust me given how vulnerable you feel." Would earn a scoff. "Given the losses and alienation in your family it must be difficult believing that communication is possible." A sneer. I felt as if a barrier existed

> between us that would transform each of my interpretations into senseless jokes – or worse.
>
> Then I thought of the strange and evocative artwork that he sometimes brought me. "Outsider" art, his work often reflected the psychotic fantasies that distracted and troubled him in the sessions. I realized the conflict that this dialectic between outside and inside stirred up in him. I was part of the inside, the social work, the world of school and family. He was on the outside, alone, but also unique and creative – special. "I have It", he would sometimes say, pointing out the powerful role that his creative "outsider" self played in his life.
>
> Seeing this I was able to use my anxiety to address this conflict between inside and outside. In particular it was hard to engage the world if it meant abandoning this sense of specialness to be "inside" with others – with me. Although this in no way resolved Henry's dilemma, it did identify why his ability to deal with the dialectic creatively was so difficult. It also opened up a path to engage him through the naming of the position that we found ourselves in.

The anxiety and sense of being stuck that I felt with Henry reflected the creative crisis that I was in with him. My self-experience was fragile and in particular my sense of my analytic self was fragmented and devitalized. In desperation I struggled to engage him through many efforts to interpret, but to no avail. In the end it was less the content and more the experience of separateness that inspired me. It was not until I identified the dilemma of "inside and outside" that I was able to organize the analytic process (and analytic self) around what appeared to me a meaningful transference interpretation. Once the words were arrived at I was able to organize further interpretations that allowed us to move forward, not necessarily towards resolution but at least we were able to identify the dialectic and the issues that blocked a creative solution to our impasse. In the end, the quality of my analytic self-experience remained tenuous at best, but for a time this allowed me to feel comfortable as I waited, unintrusively and patiently for further developments in the intersubjective field.

Creative psychoanalysis invariably involves the capacity for and acceptance of self-crisis. The analyst feels confused, doubtful, anxious, lost, etc., indicating disorganization and vulnerability. These crises may be brief and of low intensity, or extended and deeply troubling. Self-experience is repaired after effort is expended to restore the dislocation of inner subjectivity and external subjectivity embodied in the mutually determined fantasies of the transference/countertransferential field. In other words the patient and analyst both long for a selfobject experience in the midst of failure. Restoration for the analyst involves the successful reconciliation of the critical self and the self of the potential selfobject tie. He or she must seek a way of being with the patient in which the threatened tie and the associated experience of the analytic self are attuned to the selfobject needs active within the intersubjective field.

Phase 2: Resonance

> Once the artist begins to experience a growing conjunction of feeling and image the second phase begins. During this phase the feeling that the artwork is beginning to take form excites the artist. There is an increased feeling of self-cohesion, effectiveness, and vitality. The artist feels in sync with the artwork, and there is a sense of resolution in which the artwork seems to become the perfect reflection of the artist's inner life. I use the term "aesthetic resonance" for this phase.
>
> (Hagman, 2002, p. 286)

Usually after a good deal of work, in which the medium is given a form that expresses aspects of her vision and subjectivity, the analyst experiences a feeling of aesthetic resonance. This is the elusive selfobject experience that is at the heart of the psychological drive to create. Through effort and skill the artist has brought about a selfobject tie that confirms, delineates and vitalizes self-experience. Especially when the artist has been successful in relining the formal expression of subjectivity, the artwork elevates the self and mirrors the artist's grandiosity at the same time as it exhibits its own ideal nature. It is truly a complete and compelling selfobject experience.

The analytic self is mirrored in the patient's gaze, communications and modes of relating as well as the unfolding interactions and communications between them. A particular organization of the analytic self has crystallized out of the intersubjective field and could be even said to exist in the shared psychological reality of the treatment. Of course this manifestation of the analytic self only "exists" in dialogue and is therefore illusionary and subject to the variations, even disruptions, of the transference-countertransference field.

However, that being said, both analyst and patient experience the resonance as a confirming selfobject tie.

> Dan, a 35-year-old man in analytic treatment, had been abandoned by his mother at the age of 8 and left with his father, a good father but who was often away at work. Dan was beset by anxiety and self-doubt. He would often spend weekends struggling with unrealistic fears about himself and his young family. These worries improved as we explored their connection to his loss of his mother and sense of continual vulnerability.
>
> At the beginning of one session Dan noted how difficult it was to begin. That he always felt uncertain about what to take about. In particular he noted how he felt that he always had to have something interesting to offer me, otherwise I would be bored. He believed that it must be agony to meet with him and that I must be understandably fed up with him.
>
> I was not aware of any frustration on my part, but I did note that there was always a tense apprehension about the sessions, as if we were working very hard and a sense of relief at the end of each session. I could also see in his gaze the look of the young boy watching his mother pack her bags and leave

> the house. He saw me also as ready to "book", that there was nothing holding me. That even as he worked hard to entertain me, this was never enough.
>
> "Based on your experience it must be hard to believe that you have anything to offer me, that there is any reason for me to want to be with you. Your mother left. The one person you felt you could trust to want to be with you, just up and leaves. It must have shaken your confidence that anyone would stay, stay to be with you." He was listening intently. "You know the fact is I feel the opposite. I often feel very engaged and look forward to our sessions."
>
> He was shocked, and smiled. "That makes me feel good, but I find it hard to believe, as if you are just saying that. That I can't really believe that it could be true." This led to a very helpful discussion of the tension he felt between trusting me and assuming that I was no different than his mother. In fact the risk of trust was too great. If he trusted me, he would be disappointed again and lose all hope of change. However my engagement with him challenged him to see it differently, or at least consider the possibility.

I saw in his anxious, depressed gaze an image of me as his mother, packing my bags and leaving him for good. He saw me as someone so self-centered and demanding that there was no way to satisfy me. Noting this, I introduced another version of myself. In an effort to perturb the transference I challenged the assumptions upon which his approach to me was based. I engaged with the transference and induced a creative dilemma for him to struggle with. The possibility that I could be trusted existed, but had to be reconciled with the memory of the past and his present assumption that he had nothing to offer me. This creative tension encouraged change over the next few sessions. He became more forthright about his fears at the start of each session, and we began to address and work on the transference in a more effective way. The emotional tone at this point became more relaxed and positive in tone. I felt myself more effective as his analyst and he was much relieved when he realized that he could at least discuss his fears, if not, for now, change them. As a result a mutual selfobject tie, a sense or resonance developed which strengthened the treatment relationship and greatly reduced the anxiety that he had been struggling with.

But resonance is not enough. At the core of the creative analytic process is dialectic between the inner self of the analyst and the externalization of analytic subjectivity, which has become part of the subjective world of the patient. The means by which the analyst externalizes the analytic self is through interpretation. The patient responds to the interpretation, transforming it and reconciling its meaning to her own unique self-organization.

Phase 3: Failure and restoration – transmuting externalization

> Creative people tend to alternate during periods of creative work and phases when they are convinced it has not values.
>
> (Kohut, 1985, p. 114)

> The artist inevitably experiences the selfobject tie with the artwork as elusive, precarious or broken. The artist is repeatedly disillusioned regarding the artwork's perfection. He seeks to strengthen or restore the selfobject tie through its gradual refinement; by this means the work is moved closer to a formal ideal.
>
> (Hagman, 2000, p. 291)

For the artist creative work inevitably leads to the experience of failure and disruption of aesthetic resonance. This results in experiences of selfobject failure and self-crisis. The creative artist is able to manage the anxiety and/or depression during this phase, and as a result he or she reassesses the artwork, restores inspiration and takes action to develop/alter the artwork so as to restore the sense of aesthetic resonance and thus resolve the self-crisis. The alteration of the artwork so that it becomes more resonant with subjective experience is referred to as *transmuting externalization.* In other words, unlike the restoration of self through the accrual of self-structure (transmuting internalization) it is the elaboration and refinement of the external object, the artwork, that results in the resolution of self-crisis. It is this process that is the true engine of creativity, as crisis is followed by restoration through aesthetic action, something new and beautiful is articulated and given form.

Similar to the creative artist the analyst's self-experience is subject to innumerable disruptions as a result of failures in resonance and the subsequent doubts about the analytic self. This self-state must be resolved and becomes the primary motivation for the analyst's most creative work. Rather than falling back onto safer ground to try to restore what was lost (often in impossibility) the analyst must extend his or her imagination, feelings and rationality in an effort to reestablish the empathic connection that was lost, or at least threatened. Most importantly the analyst considers the transference-countertransference field, seeking to identify those aspects of the analyst's self that may have catalyzed the set of responses at the heart of the impasse. We look and feel our way into the patient's experience to try to encounter ourselves and thereby know how our patient is experiencing us. It is the patient's experience of us that becomes the reference point, the fulcrum for the next interventions, our efforts to restore the selfobject tie. Unless we can feel and/or see ourselves in the patient's gaze we are operating in the dark.

> Jim had been in analytic treatment with me for five years. He had grown up as an only child in a family troubled by anger, periodic physical abuse and depression. Jim had made a good deal of progress and had been feeling optimistic and engaged with life. His wife, on the other hand, continued to be depressed and refused to engage with him in playful activities. After several months of positive gains, Jim came in and complained that he was depressed. "I guess it's because of my marriage. I spoke to her and told her that I was depressed also. I hoped that it would help her to listen to me, to take me seriously. But then I told her we had a lot to be grateful for, happy about. She

> said I didn't understand her – that it was chemical." Jim slouched down and spoke of his relationship to his parents and his failed efforts to obtain what he needed from them.
>
> I felt distant, disconnected from him. The reflection on his failed family appeared to be too pat and too easy an explanation. The tension and vitality of the intersubjective field felt flat and listless. The vital connection that had characterized our work over the past weeks seemed absent. I wondered out loud:
>
> "You know Jim, I wonder if your depression is connected to your effort to join with your wife. To avoid the risk of expecting more from her, and maybe yourself. There is something comfortable about the depression and the memories of how your parents failed you. That there is a risk of being to connected to me, a danger in expecting to be more alive." Then I asked him. "What would happen if you weren't depressed, if you approached your wife with the expectation of engaging her in a positive way?" He looked at me with a slight hint of excitement: "It might be a catastrophe." As we talked about the risks involved in feeling more alive and expectant, his depression lifted and there was an increasing excitement in his voice. The selfobject tie was restored and the intersubjective field took on a more vital and interesting feel. "I guess it is better not to live, than be alone."

What I described in the session above was a crisis in creativity. Jim retreated to a position in which depression and creative suppression served both to maintain attachment to a depressed loved one and protect against the risk of being alive. The flatness and pat nature of his self-interpretation marked a withdrawal from creative engagement with me. As the analyst I felt a crisis, a choice between staying with Jim's depressed memory and self-experience, or actively interpreting his behavior and perturbing the self-organization. I could have chosen the path of low risk in which an acceptable exploration of memory and a damaged self would substitute for a more creative, imaginative and liberating challenge to his self and self-in-relation. By the end of this session I could see myself in his gaze, alive and engaged with Jim in a shared creative effort.

Termination

Can the psychology of the creative process help us to understand the process of psychoanalytic termination? In the following quote I discuss the point at which the tension of the creative dialectic is resolved and the self-crises that has troubled and motivated the creative artist subsides. The new artwork mirrors the restored self and is no longer an object of longing.

> Matisse when asked when he knew that a piece of artwork was finished explained: When it expresses emotion as completely as possible. It is at that point when the sense of resonance is enduring and durable. The artist

> assessing the work does not experience anxiety, depression, or fragmentation but sureness, calm or boredom. The artist no longer feels compelled to change the work because it feels balanced and complete. The work is done. It exists as a thing in itself.
>
> (Hagman, 2000, p. 290)

As the analyst and patient approach the end of a psychoanalytic treatment the nature of the creative process changes; the analyst's sense of self becomes relatively stable and cohesive. There is often a pleasant and comfortable recognition that the analytic process has been successful and the analytic self-experience is mirrored consistently from session to session, with some variations and disruptions within a manageable range. At this point the high level of creativity that characterized the heart of the analytic treatment is absent. The capacity of the patient to engage creatively with the world is restored. For both parties the relationship has begun to serve mature selfobject functions. The need for the analytic partnership is over. The patient, no longer tyrannized by transference and self-crises, is now capable of moving flexibly between relationships and the changing multiplicity of healthy selfhood. Despite the positive feelings the creative analyst begins the process of termination and looks to other analytic relationships to challenge, risk and restore her sense of the analytic self.

Recommendations to enhance analytic creativity

The following are some recommendations that I believe may enhance an analyst's creativity.

1. Cultivate a diverse and flexible sense of your analytic self. The more fixed our sense of ourselves as analysts is, and the more sure we are of our professional approach, the less responsive we will be to the special self-organization that the patient brings to treatment. The greatest benefit of the new psychoanalytic plurality is the increased range of therapeutic approaches within the analytic umbrella – thus we can better match treatment to patient.
2. Start each session in a responsive state of mind. Although we can never step out of context and our subjectivity is truly irreducible, we can take a physical and emotional position which is receptive and attentive – if we cannot, for example if we find ourselves stiff and apprehensive, guarded, we need to note this and rather than trying to "stop it" allow our self-experience to become part of what we are attentive to.
3. The psychological disorganization and reorganization that accompany creative analytic work are stressful for the analyst. In particular the loss of the selfobject function of analytic activities resulting from empathic failure or other disruptions of the clinical relationship, results in self-crisis and distressful affects. A creative analyst recognizes the opportunities that accompany

crisis and disruption. The most creative work occurs in the restoration of the analytic self.

4. Be aware of the changing nature of our experience of ourselves as analysts. This is at the beginning of a session often a vague and perhaps confused experience, as we engage the patient. During the session we find a gradually developing sense of ourselves as analysts that is particular to the unique subjectivity of our patient. The analytic self becomes constructed out of the intersubjective field and thus becomes an important analytic object – the third.
5. Be attentive to the tensions and perhaps conflicts that characterize our self-experience and the way our subjectivity (primarily manifest through interpretations) is assumed into the organizational world of the patient's subjective experience. We engage the patient as we engage ourselves within the intersubjective field.
6. Creativity is an emergent phenomenon; it is not controlled or arranged by us. We become most creative as we engage the patient's subjectivity as it is impacted by our own, moving the organization of the intersubjective field, toward new levels of organization.
7. Out of this dialectic between internal and external a fresh organization of subjective experience crystallizes.
8. Do not mistake the dramatic and often shocking enactments that can characterize certain phases of the analytic process for creativity. They are just some of the more visible and dramatic enactments that often occur as the persistent creativity of day-to-day analytic work unfolds.

Chapter 7

Creative analysis

Several minutes late, Ed (a 25-year-old Irish Catholic gay man) rushes into my office and sits down. He comments on the warmth of the chair, and speculates about the body heat of its most recent occupant. He laughs and says: "Boy I have a lot to tell you. What a week. You will definitely be angry with me. Maybe not angry – disappointed. I saw both Edward and Travis. Just what you told me not to do. But I did it."

I am tempted to comment, but I don't. I nod and let him continue uninterrupted. It is just like the artist's first brush of paint on canvas. A splash with a particular edge, a color, a texture. The canvas, up to that point stretched and unblemished, is now irrevocably changed by Ed's subjectivity.

He pauses, perhaps briefly surveying, judging his first gesture, but not too much – no judgment yet.

"I went out with both of them. I wanted to. What alternative have I anyway? I know you have been encouraging me to see other guys – to open up the net – those guys I did the hike with, but I just wanted to go out. I know Jim is an asshole, but he called and asked me to a football game. I thought. Hell, why not?"

"But you think I would not approve?"

"Well, last time you said I should dump these guys. They are no good for me. I know."

In 1949 George Braque wrote:

> A picture is an adventure each time. When I tackle the white canvas I never know how it will come out. This is the risk you must take. I never visualize the picture in my mind before starting to paint. On the contrary, I believe that the picture is finished only after one has completely effaced the idea that was there at the start.
>
> (Braque in Protter, 1997, p. 210)

With the initiation of an artwork, the successful creative artist engages in a complex and demanding psychological process. That which is subjective is externalized, and a new type of object is born – a subjective object – an artwork. As he or she adds more paint to the canvas, notes to the page, words to the screen, additional lines and color, perhaps, a meaningful form begins to crystallize. Most importantly the proto-artwork begins to acquire its own nature, a meaning outside and new to the artist. It is never quite what he or she intended – and in a sense the artwork quickly begins to speak back. In response the artist adjusts his expectations and his choices are, henceforth, partially determined by the emerging artwork itself. This dialogue between internal and external dimensions of the artist's subjectivity is at the heart of the creative process (Hagman, 2005).

Just as the artist externalizes and works on his or her subjectivity through art, the patient and analyst co-construct an intersubjective reality, often viewed as a form of theater, or dance. Thus the transference–countertransference relationship by enacting the internal fantasy life of the patient (and analyst) is an opportunity for reflection, new understandings and change. But for many of our patients life is empty of potential, and the future is only the sad, painful replication of the present and the past. Unlike the artist described above, many of our patients have an impaired capacity for *creative living* (see Winnicott, 1970, on *the ability to create the world*). Rather than embracing new experiences, they reconstruct that which is familiar and safe, despite how frustrating and painful it may be. On the other hand the analyst is oriented towards change, and the future. Nonetheless, he must for a time (perhaps quite a long time) become immersed in the experience of stuckness, listening and understanding the sources of the patient's hopelessness and paralysis. Patiently, the analyst nurtures the potential for creativity, hoping that the patient finds in the analytic process an opportunity for growth and change.

> Ed and I have being working together for five years. He is a bright, thoughtful and motivated patient. For the first several years he would work hard to portray himself as a victim, deserving of the rejection and ill treatment that he described in numerous vignettes of abusive bosses and rejecting lovers. As with many artists Ed, my patient, is stuck in a non-creative, rigid pattern in which the structure and aesthetics were always bleak and edged with self-hatred and depression. His is a vivid, compelling story, but the inability to engage life creatively, or allow himself to play with and elaborate his own sense of self is familiar.

In this chapter I will explore the vicissitudes of creativity in psychoanalysis and suggest some characteristics of creative analysis and ways that analysts can encourage and enhance the potential of patients. To do this I will compare aspects of artistic creativity with similar processes in analytic treatment. Creativity is the production of something new whatever that might be: a piece of art, an idea or an object, or a display of emotion. But for therapeutic purposes that isn't enough: for creativity to matter it must be new but also valuable, contributing to the patient's self-transformation and the accomplishment of positive, meaningful outcomes (Renik, 2001). More generally we know that happiness and effective living (the ultimate goals of analysis) requires the capacity for adaptation and change in response to new, sometimes unexpected and/or unwanted demands of environmental, social and personal realities. The ability to respond to the world creatively not only increases the probability of survival but also may enhance living conditions and emotional satisfactions.

Psychopathology as disorders of creativity

Let me start by reviewing the definition of artistic creativity which we have discussed at length in earlier chapters. Art is a psychological process that a person engages in as part of a special type of interaction with the world. During the initial phase of the creative process the artist invests the world with subjectivity – he does this with a particular type of gesture (e.g. a swipe of paint on a canvas, a written phrase, a series of notes, etc.) which marks the world with the unique signature of the artist. This new element, the artist's externalized subjectivity, becomes the focus of his creative attention and work. Susanne Langer similarly describes how the artist creates "expressive form, or apparent forms expressive of human feeling". This process becomes art when the artist engages the artwork in a dialectic during which inner and outer subjective elements interact and change each other – gesture follows and builds on the previous gesture, the artwork gradually crystallizing as a network of gestures. The direction of change in the artwork is always towards perfecting, or "making special". As a result of this the artist's subjectivity is expressed, elaborated and refined.

Artists struggle with obstacles to creativity. Lack of talent, limitations of imagination, confusion, doubt and fear, plague every artist at some time. Maybe it is just a feeling, simple and horrible at the same time, of being "blocked". He or she feels unproductive, stuck in a rut, unable to find a new approach, or a way out. Similarly our analytic patients suffer from disorders in creativity (Summers, 2005). They are, to use Adam Phillips phrase "failed artists of their lives." (1998, p. 1) Patients are unable to change frustrating behaviors, they are preoccupied with repetitive and unwanted thoughts or feelings, and they feel trapped in painful, unproductive relationships. (It is as if an artist, after sketching an ugly, unsatisfying image, cannot see any way to alter it and then finds himself repeating the repulsive image endlessly.) However, despite this, patients are not always looking for something new, or an opportunity to feel and live differently (as we have noted earlier, they often fear change). This failure of creativity is concretized in the repetitive dimensions of the transference (Stolorow and Atwood, 1992) – a familiar mode of relating and giving meaning which is unconsciously organized, derived from past experience and most importantly self-restricting.

> Ed's father died when he was thirteen and he was left with his mother, a depressed and dependent woman, and his self-involved older brother. Soon after the loss they moved to a new city and Ed lost his friends and his lifestyle which had been comfortable and reassuring. In the aftermath of these traumas

> Ed began to elaborate a set of beliefs which increased both certainty and security. Unfortunately these ideas about himself, as ineffectual, dependent and rigidly attached to his mother and her world view, had recently resulted in disruption and doubt as he tried to construct an adult life. The demand for greater independence and personal resourcefulness came into conflict with how he had for decades, come to organize and give meaning to his life.

Patients like Ed seek analysis when the approaches which they have used to cope with and manage their lives no longer work for them. These may be disrupted by life events, maturation or countless other factors. This state of inner crisis can result in a retreat from creativity, reentrenchment and stasis. At first Ed did not want to throw off the psychological chains which bound and strangled his development, rather he attempted to reassert them, seeking a way to continue on the same course without conflict or disruption – he wanted relief without change. Like many other patients, Ed's passivity, pessimism and complacency reflected his loss of a sense of his future, an inability to live in what Frank Summers (2005) calls "the future-perfect tense". This lost faith in the future devoid of potential, added to his paralysis and despair. That being said if Ed were completely hopeless he probably would not have sought therapy in the first place; perhaps his ambivalence and pain was an opportunity for change

Creative psychoanalysis

> Psychoanalysis aims to restore the artist in the patient, the part of the person that makes interest despite the early environment. At its most extreme, for the artist of her own life, it is not so much a question of what she has been given but of what she can make of what she has been given.
>
> (Adam Phillips, 1998, p. 4)

Artists work in a potential space, a transitional domain within which the psychological and the real interact, creating the conditions for something new (Winnicott, 1971). This is where imagination can have an optimal level of freedom and action is infused with fantasy, hope and desire. Similar to art, psychoanalysis involves the externalization of subjectivity. We co-construct a special reality, the analytic relationship, which is as purely subjectively determined as possible. In both art and analysis we seek to cultivate and protect that psychological space, hence the various technical constraints that we associate with good practice. In this potential space (Winnicott, 1971) of the analytic situation, patients seek to externalize their subjective experience in hopes that something might be done with it. In other words patients construct with the analyst a transference-countertransfenece relationship that is both subjectively and objectively real and thus psychological experience, as it is manifest in the potential space of the analytic relationship, can become the *object* of attention, analysis and elaboration. More specifically the patient seeks (like the artist) to achieve through analysis a refinement of, improvement in, and perhaps perfection of their self-experience (their fear of course is that it will be the same old painful thing). Experientially patients want to feel better, have increased self-esteem and be more effective. They want to actualize and improve themselves, in a similar sense that artists want to construct and improve their artworks.

> In the early months Ed described himself as an ascetic devoted to a life of self-sacrifice and quiet depression, including the suppression of his sexuality. He spent many sessions attempting to convince me of the inevitability of his empty life and the moral basis of his self-denial. A self-acknowledged gay man, he struggled to accept and endure the complete suppression of longing and passions. However sexual desire and romantic passion would erupt from time to time in response to the often troubled young men whom he would take under his wing. He would seek to take on a big brother like role, but slowly, inevitably desire would break through, causing him to become anxious and even more depressed.
>
> At times our sessions became a theater of abjection and frustrated longing. I was his witness and tormenter, my questions and interpretations only serving to push the barbs and cold chains deeper into his flesh. It would be wrong to just view Ed's efforts as resistance or a negative therapeutic reaction; no, Ed was doing his best to imagine a state of perfect being, in which desire and denial could be suspended in a self-state close to sainthood. He was seeking a state of perfection, even beauty – but inevitably and repeatedly the perfection of the transference would be shattered, as he arrived to sessions, distraught, overwhelmed and disrupted by some unexpected and unwanted passion.

In art, creativity is only possible after the artist has immersed him or herself in the work for a period of time. As Wordsworth noted: "Poems to which any value can be attached were never produced but by a man who, being possessed of more than the usual organic sensibility, had also thought long and deeply" (p. 82). In this case being an artist becomes not a hobby or a pastime but a crucial part of one's life and self-experience. Time, effort, risk, struggle, and other resources are invested in the artistic enterprise. Becoming knowledgeable and skillful as an artist becomes central to the artist's sense of self.

As Jonah Lehrer wrote in his recent book *Imagine: How Creativity Works*:

> The reality of the creative process is that it often requires persistence, the ability to stare at a problem until it makes sense. It's forcing oneself to pay attention, to write all night and then fix those words in the morning. It's sticking with a poem until it's perfect, refusing to quit a math question; working until the cut of a dress is just right. The answer won't arrive suddenly, in a flash of insight. Instead it will be revealed slowly, gradually emerging after great effort.
>
> (Lehrer, p. 56)

Similarly a creative analysis rarely results from a tentative or optional investment. Both analyst and patient must approach the process with seriousness and a willingness to invest time and effort. Creative analysis is possible only when the process matters deeply and the patient and analyst immerse themselves in it. This is not to deny ambivalence, or the various defenses such as withdrawal or devaluation, with which patient's protect themselves from threatening needs, fears and conflicts. Nonetheless at the heart of the creative process in psychoanalyses is the powerful significance and emotional investment in the relationship.

The artist's goal is the production of the artwork, and he or she may submit to much suffering and loss in its pursuit (the artwork can be supremely narcissistic, agonizingly uncooperative and uninterested in the artist's well-being). On the other hand the work of the analyst is the production, management and use of a relationship that is of benefit to the patient. The patient's happiness, welfare and experience of benefit are the primary objectives. This is how psychoanalysis both harnesses the creative process and decisively alters its aim. In the fine arts, the artist directs his or her effort toward the refinement of the artwork, the externalized subjective object. In psychoanalysis the patient elaborates the transference (the relational equivalent of the artwork) but the analyst redirects the patient's efforts by making sense of transference in terms of the patient's experience (by formulating interpretations), and reintroduces (mirrors) the patient's subjectivity back to the them via these interpretations. The patient's potentially creative efforts are thus tilted backward toward their own internal life, prompting reworking and further enactments which once again are interpreted and reflected back, with the added component of the analyst's elaboration of the patient's meanings and intensions. Thus transference interpretations offer the patient discrepant and hopefully transformative opportunities. It is important to note that by the term *discrepant* I do not mean only conflicting or contradictory, rather it refers to the fact that no matter how empathic or mirroring the analyst tries to be, his interpretation transforms the patient's meanings, as they are filtered through the analyst's sensibility as well as the shared subjective space of the dialogue. What the patient confronts is their own subjective experience, enhanced by the therapeutic function of the analyst and analytic process. However, the dialectic just described is inadequate to explain change. As with the artist, who is motivated not just to solve problems, but more importantly to refine and even perfect the artwork (to do their best, and "get it right"), the patient is also motivated by an affirmative drive. In other words patients, like artists, try to "do *their* best" (albeit they can seem to be bent on the opposite) and the analysis harnesses this active, affirmative urge to facilitate the process. The traditional notion of the transference, even in modern relational terms, fails to emphasize these positive strivings, in particular the way transference can reflect the search for reparation (Stolorow and Atwood, 1992), renewed development and creative experience (Winnicott, 1953; Summers, 2005; Hagman, 2010).

Marian Tolpin discussed such a progressive view of transference in her paper "Compensatory structures: Paths toward the restoration of the self" (1997). There she argued that the tendency of psychoanalysis to limit the understanding of transferences to childhood sources, resistance, or organizations of meaning has resulted in a misunderstanding of more mature developmental strivings as well as the healthy motivation to seek out and make use of relationships that can repair and/or enhance self-experience. According to Tolpin this "forward-edge" of transference reflects the patient's active search for recovery by turning away from old, failed relationships, seeking new experiences that can resolve conflict and/or compensate for or repair deficits.

In Tolpin's later paper "Doing psychoanalysis of normal development: Forward edge transferences" (Tolpin, 2002) she expanded on this idea:

> The deepest layer of the psyche consists of strivings of the forward edge – once normal needs of the unmirrored self, of the self that is chronically enfeebled and/or fragmenting and is in search of idealized strengths, of expanding alikeness experiences with a kindred soul. It is the reactivation of these needs in selfobject transferences that is potentially transforming – the needs and the therapist's responses to them can revitalize the self, restore the urge to complete development, and get development back on track.

Terms like "striving", "search" and "urge" imply a new understanding of the patient's creativity. In her discussion of Matt (Egan and Kernberg, 1984), Tolpin described a young man's search for a new relationship to help him break free from a lifetime of self-denigration and to resume his thwarted emotional development. Later in the paper, after the analysis has addressed earlier failures and established an adequate mirroring transference, Tolpin noted:

> Matt was no longer so entirely alone and lonely in his splendid isolation – his process established a self-selfobject transference that reinstated phase-expectable encouragement, mirroring and guidance. The analyst was a "usable selfobject" if you will and Matt was enabled to make use of his multiple development-enhancing functions, including his function of interpretation.
>
> (Tolpin, p. 184)

For Tolpin the "forward edge" of any transference expresses the patient's healthy attempts to solve problems, seek opportunities and bring about changes that can create new relationships and restore a damaged sense of self. The analyst's role is to provide the context in which opportunities for reparative experiences are made available and in which the patient feels able to satisfy developmental needs and affiliative longings. From this perspective patients are not just passive recipients of developmentally needed responses, but creative people, striving to find satisfaction and opportunities to fulfill themselves. The role of the analyst is to attend to the relational context, interpret any anxieties related to the experience and expression of personal activities and interests; and finally to identify and support the patient's efforts to renew development and accomplish his or her psychological and relational ambitions.

Even seemingly destructive and negative behaviors can have an affirmative aspect. In this light Roy Schaefer wrote about the analyst's need to understand and respond to the dual nature of patient's transferences:

> I am referring to the ways that these negative-seeming self-presentations are, unconsciously, elements of a grand strategy both for protecting oneself in the infantile danger situations that, unconsciously, have remained as real as ever and for *making the most of oneself in one's relations with others* . . . these productions must be viewed from the vantage point of *personal action or goal directed activity*, if not the analyst only sets limits to their analyzability.
>
> (Schaefer, 1983)

In other words, for Schaefer the analyst must analyze the relationship that exists between the patients efforts both to protect and preserve oneself and the effort to "make the most" out of one's relation to others. These interpretations of the patient's "personal action and goal directed activity" support the discovery of new solutions.

But, as Schafer noted, a person may not be consciously interested in being creative, he or she may seek improvement down the same old pathways, repeating patterns that are familiar and safe – not necessarily new. (This in fact is also true of most artists – creativity is not a necessary feature of artistic work.) The analytic environment offers an alternative: at first inviting the patient to construct a situation that he or she feels safe with, the analyst artfully and repeatedly identifies discrepancies, challenging the solution and urging the patient toward unknown and perhaps surprising new meanings.

In other words, analysis is an ongoing sequence of interactions in which the patient actualizes his or her subjective life in an environment which encourages self-expression, elaboration and change. Of course the patient's experience of their subjectivity has many dimensions, meanings and degrees of accessibility to conscious awareness, judgment, and ultimately, potential revision. The analyst's role is to both resonate with and resist the patient's efforts, offering opportunities for new understanding and new experience. At the heart of this process is a series of dialectics in which the patient's subjectivity interacting with the analyst's subjectivity is perturbed, resulting in conflicts and tensions which may necessitate a new response.

> I found the beauty that Ed was seeking to be dull and stale. It lacked complexity and certainly had none of the richness that Ed would show during his moments of humor or impishness. As Ed's analyst I did two things: (1) I interpreted the way in which he expected me to lose hope in him and that our failure would only reassert his self-denial; (2) I highlighted the passionate nature of his search for sexual contact, and the way in which he tried to

> suppress the desire which was so important to him. In fact it wasn't so much sex that mattered but the inhibition of his search for self-actualization and his fear of asserting himself, not just in sex, but work, play and family relations. In this way I began to conjure another image of Ed, gay, assertive and passionate, and would hold it up to him, next to his selfimage of the monk which he clung to and nurtured.

There is a difference between reacting to the other (which can be a highly conservative and repetitive process) and creating something new. Reactivity is often based on patterns, or schemata, which impose on ambiguity a fixed meaning and allows the patient to prepare for expected failure or injury (Bromberg, 2006). Newness by definition cannot be anticipated; it is unexpected and violates our prior expectations. In the best of cases it disarms us and stimulates innovation. Creativity in psychoanalysis crystallizes out of innumerable interactions – the Boston Charge Group refers to this rich, complexity as "sloppiness". There is no way that such a process can be controlled. In fact creativity arises as a result of this complexity, and the changing impact of conscious intention, unconscious meanings and motives, and the tendency of this complex system to spontaneously reorganize. Making use of these unexpected moments (what the Boston Change Group refer to as *now* moments (Stern *et al.*, 1998)) requires that the analyst cultivate a responsive, improvisational stance, characterized by an attitude of freedom and lack of constraint. Lichtenberg (1999) referred to this as *disciplined spontaneous engagement* in which the analyst responds spontaneously and unexpectedly, even while continuing to be anchored to their professional role. However, in analysis as in art, preparation and readiness is often crucial to the exploitation of the unexpected.

> For several months Ed was lost in a funk. Unhappy and frustrated, he clung to routines and states of mind which, albeit miserable, were familiar and safe. However, the fruits of our sessions had led to moments of intense dissatisfaction and the horrible recognition that he was wasting his life. One day, while jogging near his home, he was struck by a bicycle and knocked to the ground. Shaken emotionally more than physically hurt, he had the sudden feeling that he had had it, that he needed to do things differently, that he could no longer deny his desire for change. In his next session he was anxious but energized. He felt ready to begin to work with me on change.

Artists are always on the lookout for the accidental or strange, hoping to discover something that might be useful. They may cultivate *divergent* thinking in which the spontaneous and unanticipated are valued and made use of. Similarly, for patients like Ed unexpected events may challenge old assumptions. But for the opportunity to result in change, work of a different type may be needed. Moments of chaos often heighten the tension between old and new, and hopefully as with Ed the balance shifts toward the new. Then the patient and analyst must identify, highlight and mold these possibilities selecting those feelings, ideas and fantasies that have value, meaning that they meet the patient's needs and increase the probability of more effective living, improved self-experience and happiness.

Let me sum up what we have said so far. As in art, the psychotherapeutic process results in co-constructed, externalized subjective "objects". In other words, transferences and enactments, in which the inner life of the patient is placed outside the self, independent from intrapsychic reality. However the transference is never just a duplicate of inner fantasy. Inevitably when fantasy makes contact with reality (the patient's subjectivity interacting with the analyst's subjectivity) both are changed. Like the artist who is challenged by the independent subjectivity of the artwork which he or she has constructed (which is now separate and distinct from the self), the patient struggles with the new meanings that have been elaborated in dialogue with the analyst. These now externalized meanings must be reconciled with inner responses, and a dialectic between inner and outer subjectivity occurs. The patient confronts disparate aspects of self-experience that are now concretely present between him and the analyst. This tension increases the probability of new meanings and new modalities of relatedness and self-experience. With adequate preparation and assistance, this psychological state may be an opportunity for reorganization and the elaboration of something new. This probability is increased when the analyst offers the patient a vision of his or her potential self at the moment it can be of use. In this way the analyst's intervention can break the dialectical logjam prompting the patient to create something new.

> A central component of analysis is the recognition and continued working through of the patient's defenses against the realization of possibilities contained in the analyst's vision of the patient.
>
> (Summers, 2005)

Believing in the possible

Artists are experts in the management, manipulation and exploitation of the possible. Through experience and skill honed through practice, they confront the ambiguous, confusing and unexpected in an effort to bring some type of organization and meaning into the world. Part of this process involves a sense of what is emergent, perhaps latent, in the artwork. In other words the artist needs to believe (at least some of the time) that the artwork has potential. Some artists may have a pretty clear idea of where they are going and what they want from the work, others may be just one step ahead, holding a feeling or image of what the work may become which is vague, ineffable and emotionally complex. Trust in oneself, resilience and persistence are important qualities in successful artists, faced with uncertainty, doubt and the ever-present possibility of failure. But always there is a premonition, some feeling of what the artwork in process might be evolving into. This feeling or image is a guide; it helps the artist coax the work towards completion.

Similarly, how can the patient believe in a self which is only a possibility? In his paper "On the therapeutic action of psychoanalysis" (1960) Hans Loewald explained how the analyst holds in mind visions of the patient's potential, which are not who the patient is, but who he might become. Of course this "reflection" of the patient's nascent self is not fixed, or predictive. The analytic interaction is continually molding and sculpting this potential self. As Summers noted "The therapist forms and reforms this vision in accordance with the emergence of the patient's material" (p. 59). Rather it is what the patient comes up against, reflected as if in some strange new mirror, prompting him to react, and adjust his self-image and the habitual modes which he has relied on to cope with both inner and outer realities. Lawrence Friedman (1988) noted the importance of such identification in development and analysis. He wrote:

> One childhood need which is fulfilled in analysis is the need to identify with one's own growth potential as seen in the eyes of the parent. Being reacted to like that not only provides hope but structures reality in a relevant and promising manner. The analyst must accept the patient on his own terms, and at the same time not settle for them. If he does not accept the patient on his own terms, it is as though he is asking him to be someone else, the patient will not have cause for hope, and he will not recognize the analyst's vision. If the analyst settles for the patient's terms, he is betraying the patient's wish for greater fulfillment.
>
> (pp. 27 and 34)

Additionally the patient's experience of the analyst's "reflection" is not accurate, the patient does not actually know what the analyst is thinking, or what the analyst intends to do with this understanding (an understanding in any case that is always ambiguous, changeable and colored by the analyst's subjectivity – the Boston Change group refers to this quality as *fuzzy intentionalizing*), but it is different enough from his own self-experience to provoke a state of psychological tension that may encourage creative change. It is both through innumerable interactions as well as the analyst's attitude toward the patient, that an "image" of a potential self crystallizes in the mind of the analyst, and then in the dialogic space. Loewald described this process:

> As in sculpture, we must have, if only in rudiments, an image of that which needs to be brought into its own. The patient, by revealing himself to the analyst, provides rudiments of such an image through all the distortions – an image which the analyst has to focus in his mind, thus holding it in safe keeping for the patient to whom it is mainly lost. It is this tenuous reciprocal tie which represents the germ of a new object relationship.
>
> (Loewald, 1960, p. 17)

For Loewald the patient's creativity is restricted by the way in which the unconscious mind is cut off from the opportunities offered by present reality and most importantly the future. Defensive operations and structures serve to block the internalization and integration of higher levels of self-organization offered by the interaction with the environment mediated by the preconscious. In psychoanalysis the emergence of the transference and the introduction of the analyst's interpretations create the possibility for "freer interplay between unconscious and preconscious systems, whereby the preconscious retains its originality and intensity, lost to the unconscious in repression, and the unconscious regains access to the capacity for progression in the direction of higher organization" (Loewald, 1960, p. 25). However, this integrative process is not easy. The tension which Loewald described between the unconscious and preconscious, or between the neurotic compromises and new object relation is characterized by anxiety, fear of disorganization and ambivalence, as much as it is by positive feeling and hope.

Similarly, artistic work involves a fluctuation between states of anxiety and doubt, and clarity and confidence (Kohut, 2007; Hagman, 2000). The artist's creativity depends on the ability and strength to move effectively between these states in the process of seeking resolution. However, the work of the analyst is to promote the elaboration of a therapeutic matrix (or creative context) within which the patient experiences both tension and safety. To do this the analyst must simultaneously perturb and assure the patient. Creativity cannot occur in the midst of too much fear and anxiety; this often results in reentrenchment and the fortification of reliable defenses. *Change requires disruption in the context of safety*: the patient must be "safe but not too safe" (Bromberg, 2006, p. 189) He wrote further that "The goal is to pro-vide sufficient safety so that the patient can make it back from the edge of the abyss and be aware of having done so." The patient's psychic status quo must be disturbed in a way that he or she can respond with new solutions, but new solutions are hard to develop in the face of uncertainty and perhaps threat – unless there is preparation, a readiness for change and the facilitative presence of the analyst.

> Ed began to alternate between his reliance on old forms and his creation of his new self. At times he was the self-abjuring monk, at others the lusty gay man. For a long time the relative risks of each image was of major concern. For a long time the "new man" whom he might become was also threatening, not just from guilt but the recognition that his being "out" might disrupt relationships which had been central to his life. His creation of his new self had to await his working out the value of change. In our sessions we explored at length and repeatedly both the fears which held him back, the thrilling opportunities of his new life and the inner vision of himself as empowered, passionate and ambitious. Therefore his creative work was not only in becoming his new self, but also in giving himself value and meaning. Pursuing a life of ambition and passion was increasingly important, and with time he began to idealize what he worked for as a person, and he began to seek relationships which might add value to his life.

Enhancing the analyst's creative readiness

From the perspective of systems theory, creativity is a quality of complex systems that experience periodic spontaneous reorganizations as a result of perturbations arising either from within or outside the specific subsystem involved (Stolorow, 1997; Coburn, 2007, 2009). Despite its seeming simplicity, and especially if you take into account the larger context, the psychoanalytic relationship is just such a complex system. At the same time the analytic process is characterized by options and choices, the participants mold and direct the process, even as they are changed by it. Confronted by this complexity, the analyst is trained and experienced in finding threads of meaning, tendrils of hope and motivation, and formulating interventions which can urge the patient toward change. But, I ask, how can we participate in the system to maximize the probability of a creative outcome? Since we cannot and should not "control" the process, what should our stance be in the system? I believe that we can identify some general qualities of a creative analyst.

The analyst learns about the patient the way an artist learns the nature of his medium, hands-on, through trial and error. This importantly includes not just the patient as an individual but the entire analytic situation, the relationship and all its changing qualities. In this regard the analyst's theoretical and clinical model is crucial. It is through these lenses that we can be said to know the analytic situation and we act, conservatively or creatively within these models. As with the artist it is important that there are a set of values, clinical methods and vision of health for the analyst and patient to communicate and work with. However, in creative analysis the most important factor is not the general validity of any specific theory of process, but the relevance of the model to the particular analytic pair, and whether or not the model is of use. If the clinical model reflected in the analyst's actions and attitudes is not relevant to the patients subjective experience and especially if the model does not resonate with the patient's therapeutic goals (the area of forward edge strivings), then the model, and those ideas and interventions which follow from it, will not be of much use to the patient. Interpretations will fall far from their mark, despite the analyst's conviction, the patient will feel misunderstood and the process will stall (Renik, 2001, pp. 239–240). I believe models which expand possibilities and options are the best choices, those that emphasize experience and subjectivity over method and fact.

At the same time the analyst's understanding of the patient must be held lightly, it is always provisional and open to revision (Coburn, 2007, p. 12): we are constantly observing, formulating hypotheses (often vague and provisional), testing them (perhaps only in our minds), discarding many, and gradually elaborating what makes sense and seems useful. "The rules of the game change as a result of the play" Coburn noted about the ongoing emergent nature of clinical understanding (Coburn, 2007). To go one step further, the analyst must be willing to "not know" and allow the process to unfold without being sure of what is going on. At the same time he must be alert to developments that often are "sloppy", ambiguous and confusing. Winnicott referred to the importance of nonsense and formlessness in the emergence of creativity (Winnicott, 1971, pp. 55–56). In this light an intuitive approach, with a willingness to make full use of the unconscious is essential. The analyst is always only incompletely and inadequately aware, and our knowing may be far more subliminal and unconscious than we want to admit.

In a similar way that artists have to tolerate and work through periods of messiness and confusion, the analyst must allow himself to feel anxious, and be able to sit with the anxiety and make use of it to move the process forward. A healthy skepticism is crucial and a productive critical attitude in which everything is viewed as far more uncertain and complex than it appears. Affective attunement involves self-regulation and containment, as well as a readiness to make use of the countertransference. Perhaps the most difficult thing for the analyst is to maintain the openness of the analytic space. It is reassuring to find an explanation, or more specifically to identity what is "really going on" with the patient. It is hard to remain ambiguous, let alone to cultivate a quality of formlessness, out of which new possibilities might, or *might not*, emerge.

At the same time the analyst and patient must select, identifying certain themes or meanings, to be highlighted, interpreted and worked through. The analyst must be alert to the feelings, thoughts and attitudes which may herald the elaboration of new self-states and ways of being. Renik encourages the analyst, when "flying blind" to solicit as much help as possible from the patient in determining what to do (Renik, 2001). Engaging the patient as a full collaborator in the process of exploration and decision making expands the possibilities of the analytic interaction. This dialogue often brings to light aspects of the patient's changing emotional life which have been obscure. As Summers noted: "the analyst's response to fledgling states will help the patient take note of them and provide the opportunity for their becoming real" (Summers, 2005, pp. 149). The analyst's and patient's willingness to collaborate and choose in the midst of uncertainty is facilitative of the therapeutic process in and of itself. In sum creativity in analysis is both a spontaneously emergent phenomenon and the outcome of a complex set of deliberate and selective acts.

Values play an important role in choice. The analyst must hold to a general desire for the refinement and perfection of the process – despite its messiness and indeterminacy. Nonetheless, we don't just want any outcome; we are working with the patient to maximize the chance that he or she will get positive benefit from the analysis. Given this the analyst always seeks to articulate the process, to strengthen that which feels best, and to work with the patient to achieve positive results. This is hard to do in the midst of such ambiguity and uncertainty, but in the end the analyst, like the artist, is driven by a desire to get it right, to bring about something of beauty. This attitude is an important part of the positive valence of the therapeutic process. As the patient struggles, the analyst tips the situation toward health.

> Ed's struggle between the reassurance of rituals and religious belief and the sexual excitement and adventure of his potential self was productive.

Ultimately the ebb and flow between the two poles helped Ed organize himself and identify goals as he worked to develop his adult life and sense of a future. Recently he has begun to articulate a middle way as he tempers his old religious fervor with a mature sense of growing friendships with other gay men. He is more confident about his desires and his ability to negotiate passionate relationships. At the same time he has continued his participation in the religious community, albeit less compulsively and with a more ecumenical attitude. Several weeks back he was invited to attend a discussion group at a church run by another denomination. Made up of men from various Christian communities, the goal of the meeting is to help the members find a place as gay men in religious communities. His openness to this group surprised and excited him – it was something new.

Conclusion: Principles of creative analysis

> Psychoanalysis is not a search for the hidden truth about the patient and the patient's life. It is instead the emergence through curiosity and the acceptance of uncertainty, of constructions which may never have been thought before. Furthermore, these constructions are not merely sensible stabs at history and descriptions: they are part and parcel of the new world patient and analyst are creating between them.
>
> (Stern, 1983, p. 100)

1. Creative Analysis is not a treatment. It is a form of art which frees patients to believe in the future and realize the potential which may have been blocked, inhibited, denied or derailed. It is not about healing, repairing, or re-parenting (although these may be useful metaphors) it is about providing opportunities for self-creation (Summers, 2005).
2. The goal of analysis is for the patient to experience desired life changes resulting from the investigation and reorganization of experience.
3. Change in analysis is driven not by the analyst's interventions but the patient's own motivation and capacity for self-transformation (which may be blocked or suppressed at the start) and how the patient makes use of the analyst in this process.
4. The analyst's function is to understand the patient, help to identify potentials and motivations to change, and support the patient's efforts to bring about change.
5. Creative analysis is a depth psychological process (not just cognitive or behavioral) which explores the sources of the patient's resistance to self-actualization, identifies hidden potential, unrealized capacities and strengths.
6. The patient is not controlled by past experience, rather the patient's memories serve as guides to self-protection and templates for the organization of present experience, and potentially, future selves.

7. The exploration of memory is a means of understanding why the patient acts as they do in the present, and can help to identify areas of potential growth.
8. Transference is a form of action which the patient engages in with the analyst. It expresses the patient's initiative and attempt to accomplish something meaningful (however painful and repetitive it may seem).
9. The analyst facilitates the emergence of meaning and self-creation by supporting the analytic relationship as a "potential space" within which new meanings and new self-states can be constructed.
10. Countertransference is the psychological process by which the analyst comes to understand and empathize with the patient's experience – however countertransference is not just determined by the patient's past and/or current experience, but also the potential for growth and change.
11. The mutative effect of analytic interventions (interpretations, enactments, corrective experiences) is derived from the ways in which they reflect the analyst's vision of the patient's potential for generating new organizations of self-experience and the support they provide for what is emergent and active in the patient's psychological life (Summers, 2005).
12. The success of any psychoanalysis depends on the analysand's ability to make use of us. Our role is to recognize, encourage and facilitate the analysand's unique potential for creative living (Winnicott, 1971).

Chapter 8

Postscript

Creative living

Famously, Freud asserted that the goal of psychoanalysis was to allow patients to "love and work" unimpeded by the effects of neurotic suffering and its consequent restrictions to living. Sustained normal unhappiness was, to him, a desirable outcome. And that may indeed be the case for many of us; however more recently analysts have had higher expectations. In this book I have promoted the value of increased capacity for creativity and creative living as the desirable analytic objective. From this perspective effective treatment is associated with a fundamental change in the patient's relationship with both inner and outer worlds, involving the emergence of new and surprising meanings and experiences. There have been other analytic authors supporting this view among this group, Hector Juan Fiorini has written *The Creating Psyche: Theory and Practice of Tertiary Processes*. In this new volume, Dr. Fiorini (Doctor of Psychoanalysis and Professor of Psychology at the Buenos Aires University) elaborating on D. W. Winnicot's ideas of potential space and the "area of cultural development", examines the emergence of the conditions for creativity in the clash between the "unformed and empty" primary processes and the "structured, symbolizing" secondary processes. Fiorini posits tertiary processes, neither formal nor formless, in which new organizations, new experiences can emerge. In this postscript I will consider the implications of this idea for artistic creativity and most importantly the creative potential of psychoanalytic treatment.

D. W. Winnicott revealed the creative potential in all human experience. In particular he showed how inner fantasy and outer "reality" enter into relationships within a psychological zone he called potential space, which is transitional between subjective and objective realities. He demonstrated how the real mother, receiving and responding to the spontaneous gestures and projections of her child, allows for the child to experience a mix up between her real being and the dreams and longings of her child. Over time, if the mother remains confidently suspended and resonant, the child comes to take for granted the relaxed flow of influence between themselves and the world. The protective barriers, which we have discussed at length in earlier chapters, is not even considerered. There is a mutual ongoing enrichment of the child's experience of self and self-in-relationship. In the space between, the mind intermingles with the world, and something new crystallizes. The unexpected becomes as natural as a dream and as real as stone. Creative living is taken for granted, like breathing, sustaining life.

The artist enters into relationship with a reality of his or her own creation. The art work is subjectivity made objective. Psychological experience made real. This subjective object which Winnicott described becomes subject to the artist's skill and change efforts. The object is made into a more precise, more articulate, more affecting expression of the artist's aesthetic imaginings. It is worked, reworked, destroyed, rebuilt, refined, yes even perfected, so that he or she feels that it is "just right". As we have seen this process may even occur at the artist's expense – the artist at work cares for nothing but the artwork, and he or she will sacrifice what is necessary to "get it right". Because of this art is not inherently therapeutic. It may feel good, the artist may feel satisfied and experience heightened self-esteem, but nothing is changed within the artist's self-experience. He may be just as neurotic and miserable in the end as he was when he started. But – the art work was done right and it is good. That is all that matters.

Psychoanalysis evokes an objectification of the self, a subjective object, the transference. In this way a potential space is created for the analyst and analysand to work on the self, making self-experience itself the object of creative effort. What in another context might have been the art work becomes the analysand's self and the object of shared creative analytic work. The analyst offers his capacity to play in this potential space to interpenetrate and engage the analysand, offering his creative capacities to help reconfigure, elaborate and refine the analysand's self. Most importantly this process stimulates the analysand's openness to the unpredictability of potential experiencing, allowing "not-me elements" to enter into and become part of self-structure. Old restrictions and self-protections are let go, dismantled and a new, flexible interchange between self and world is enabled.

What are the processes within the potential space that lead to creation? Winnicott believed that aggression, the urge to destroy the object, created the conditions for the experience of the object's survival and "discovery/creation". In *The Creating Psyche* Fiorini has a more complex view, suggesting that the creative subject seeks not to destroy the object or the self but to disrupt the forms and assumptions which imprison them both and squelch the creative drive. He argues that the mind is driven by the need to escape the threat of imprisonment within a world of accepted forms. He postulates a "force in the creating psyche that works against the threat of capture". Fiorini believes that this "force acts like a drive, leading to the dismantling of established forms in order to move the psych into new spaces, spaces of the unknown" (Fiorini, 2014, p. 26). The resulting struggle between the parts of the psyche that cling to the familiar, structured and safe and those parts that seek disruption, disorganization and chaos is characterized by both insistence and resistance as well as the distress and fascination of freedom. The creating psyche is one which ventures into the abyss of chaos, which contains all possible forms, assembling and dissembling, appearing and disappearing, a state in which Fiorini believes "the impossible" and "the possible" coexist in dialectic tension. Another aspect of these tertiary processes is "narcissism in transit" meaning that the creating subject identifies with the creative process itself and is "willing to dynamite all identifications" (p. 42); there is a horror at being captured by identity. He or she seeks the "space of being possible" and may seek to exist (or not exist) at the boundaries between where things come together (p. 45). However, many people undergoing this experience of chaos and disruption will experience vertigo, the fear of collapsing into the abyss of nothingness, hence the ever present tendency to retreat from creative opportunities and cling to the known and familiar, the given.

> Many anxieties tempt the subject to escape, to panic, to despair or to control by traveling familiar roads to prevent the process from unfolding its potential for radical novelty. Psychopathology may take over and sidetrack the process, acting as old attractors which may arrest the process and offer it old clothes and false paths.
>
> (p. 166)

Normally the belief in "absolutisms" (what Fiorini views as givens, established forms and identifications) allows people to experience their world as safe, secure and predictable (Stolorow, 2007, p. 16) However, according to Fiorini, these assumptions are just the type of traps that confine the creative subject. On the other hand the traumatic shattering of protective absolutisms can cripple the potential for creative living. In his book *Trauma and Human Existence* Robert Stolorow wrote:

> Emotional trauma shatters absolutisms, a catastrophic loss of innocence that permanently alters one's sense of being-in-the-world. Massive deconstruction of the absolutisms of everyday life exposes the inescapable contingency of existence on a universe that is random and unpredictable and in which no safety or continuity of being can be assured . . . a vanquished sense of estrangement and solitude takes hold
>
> (p. 40)

The traumatized psyche (as opposed to the creating psyche) is plunged into the abyss, the void within which meaning is destroyed but then transformed, not into something useful and new, but into a crippling awareness of vulnerability that necessitates emergency measures to find and/or construct safety. Trauma may at times be an opportunity for creative living, but more often than not, at least for a time, flexibility, openness, playfulness are foreclosed and replaced by panic or rigid self-protectiveness. It is not what happened, but the resulting process. The traumatized subject shuns creative responses, clamping down on experience, fortifying the self which may become reified and locked into a mask of fear.

According to Fiorini creative living means the constant refusal to settle for established forms and given identities. It may even mean resisting the normal tendency to seek stability and assurance in a cohesive sense of self or social role.

Creative living eschews identifications and cultivates flexible and responsive self-experience. On the other hand it does not mean living in a state of chaos or nothingness, but it does mean being able to not only tolerate the experience of chaos, but to work with it, to explore chaos, to transform objects and self into new forms, to give order and then destroy it again and again. Creative living for Fiorini means that old distinctions, time-honored by psychoanalysts, between conscious and unconscious, feeling and word, analyst and patient, past, present and future, are allowed to be collapsed, disassembled and then reassembled in new forms to suit the special nature of each analyst relationship and process.

> In clinical practice chaos becomes visibly manifest in crises . . . with unexpected changes which paralyze and disorient. An opportunity to gestate new answers may potentially emerge, a risk of greater damage and loss is experienced above all else. It will have to be endured.
>
> (pp. 165–166)

The challenge for the analyst is to avoid interfering in the process which might foreclose the opportunity for a creative response. "Preserving contact with the self-organizing possibilities of unstable chaotic systems" (p. 165) the analyst attends to the present moment, the patient's experience in the midst of crisis. This sustained innocence combined with alertness, helps the analyst not to get in the way, but also prepares him or her to observe new directions and support the emergence of the patient's creative response. Ultimately, if the patient is not to remain in a state of panic and chaos (a non-creative place), a selection process must be engaged in, the chaos is given meaning, and new, clearer, differentiable forms crystallize out of the fragments. This is the heart of creativity to Fiorini, the crisis of chaos, accompanied with disruption and de-identification, creates an opportunity for a creative response in which new psychological forms and meanings are developed, soon to be destroyed and reconfigured in an ongoing, evolving living system. This also is the essence of creative analysis, as meaning is co-constructed, disrupted and restored in a process which frees the patient from their self-protective prison of beliefs and behaviors, eventually opening his or her psyche to the possibilities of creative living.

There are many forms of psychotherapy which are legitimate and helpful to people. Most of them are of a supportive nature, others are remedial and/or rehabilitative. They offer an opportunity for improvement in self-feeling and in the quality of the patients' social, family and work life. They are not primarily creative, and are not intended to be. If they increase the creative potential of the patient, that is an indirect benefit, not fundamental to the treatment itself. However, creativity is at the heart of the psychoanalytic process – perhaps, its defining quality. I don't mean this in terms of any particular content or treatment procedure; rather it is in the way psychoanalysis creates the conditions for the opening up of psychological life and the restoration of people's inherent capacities for creative living. How does anything truly new emerge out of the clinical process? What happens in analytic treatment that helps a patient transcend the repetitive and self-defeating strictures of their unique psychopathology? What are the conditions from which potential and possibilities emerge out of pain, frustration and fear?

The values and processes of Creative Analysis which we have explored in this book suggest that within any person, even the most stuck and miserable, there is the potential to risk something new, an urge, even drive, to confront chaos and wrest meaning out of nothingness. I would argue that under the proper conditions, with the active assistance and support of the right person (in our case the analyst), crisis can be endured, worked with and creatively transformed. Psychoanalysis with its powerful blend of passionate engagement, empathy, abstinence and thoughtful reflection, creates the conditions for transformation, a sustained experience of disruption, crisis, and reorganization, which does not necessitate an emergency response of shutting down, foreclosing and walling oneself off to life. Nor does Analysis offer an easy way out, or a predetermined method or philosophy, which reassures and provides a particular meaning as an end in itself. The process of Creative Analysis encourages the analyst to recognize the uniqueness of each analytic process and person, and to be exquisitely sensitive to his or her impact on the analysand, and most important, the way the analyst can facilitate or block the creative processes that are set in motion by the psychoanalytic situation.

Appendix

The following discussion was written for Chapter 1 as a support for the definition of art which is discussed there. I have moved it to the end of the book as an appendix because it may not be of interest to the primary audience, analysts and therapists, but may be of interest to readers who are seeking additional support for my thesis or who are just curious about the particular areas of research which are discussed here. These areas are: neuropsychology of art, the evolutionary sources of art, and the matrix of art in human attachment.

Art and the brain

> It is the imaginative capacity, the brain's ability to impose on sensory perception what it needs or wants for a picture to be made in the mind, which defines what happens in art.
>
> (Lois Oppenheim, 2005, p. 25)

> A serious long-term limitation of any strictly neuroscientific solution to our definition of art lies in the fact that the common component processes of experience in the nervous system are not the only drivers behind the experience of art. The most important drivers are largely cultural or cognitive-cultural and depend not only on what is experienced but also on interpretative algorithms that may be peculiar to individuals or societies and have no mental instantiations. These algorithms are embedded in the "distributed" cognitive processes of social networks.
>
> (Donald, 2006, p. 11)

Over the last several decades neuroscience has offered some suggestions regarding the role of brain function and structure in the production and enjoyment of art. That being said, Brown and Dissanayake (2009) (and others) have pointed out the limited applicability of much neuroaesthetic research and theorizing. Most importantly Art, or more specifically the activity of making art, involves more than perceptual preferences, modes of organization, etc. Hence the study of the brain's readiness to organize perception and integrate emotion and form has so far failed to capture the complexity of human artistic life. However, despite these limitations, some of the findings are in fact useful to us as we try to find some defining characteristics of artistic creativity and production. In particular most neuroscientists have supported the notion that the brain actively constructs perception and seeks to organize forms of experience according to some limited set of principles. Several of these theorists have begun to develop models of art as an activity of the brain and mind that seeks to organize thinking, feeling and experiencing in special ways that enhance adaptation and optimize creativity.

The neurologist Semir Zeki argues that the human brain is designed to construct a sense of order in the midst of an ambiguous and ever-changing environment. (Terrence Deacon [2006] has also discussed this perspective at length.) In particular, the brain is designed to seek out some basic forms that are common to certain situations or scenes by which it can reliably recognize and deal with future experiences. Specifically he points how the brain organizes and structures perception according to virtual lines, light wavelength ratios and motion detection to arrive at the essence of an image or perceptions. Seki argues that the brain's ability to organize itself in order to perceive the world and ultimately engage in aesthetic experiences is dependent on good enough early experiences during which the basic neurological capacities are set. In the end, the goal of the artful brain is to develop conceptual ideals, cognitive forms that are felt to capture the essence of certain expectable, familiar experiences. Artists by means of art use these brain capacities and manipulate them. "One of the functions of art is an extension of the major functions of the visual brain" (Seki, 1998).

I would argue, consistent with Seki, that artists make use of the brain's capacities to create meaningful forms of subjective experience. In this sense artists don't just want to illustrate certain brain functions but most importantly to elaborate and refine them. In fact, some neuroscientists see exaggeration or elaboration as a key component of art making and aesthetic experience, for example V. S. Ramachandran goes beyond Seki's notion of ideals to claim that the power of art comes from the function of the "peak shift".

> What the artist tries to do (either consciously or unconsciously) is to not only capture the essence of something but also to amplify it in order to more powerfully activate the same neural mechanism that would be activated by the original object.
>
> (Ramachandran, 1998, p. 17)

A peak shift occurs when an artist after having identified an essential form of an object or experience – meaning a selection of perceptual characteristics that are felt to define the object – exaggerates this form, so that the essential qualities are amplified and made more apparent. In this way the object and artwork take on a more pronounced and meaningful quality. The artwork is no longer just a representation it is an ideal, something compelling and special.

Ramachandran's point does not just apply to representational art. In fact abstract art is frequently the best example of attempts to find essences, and to exaggerate these forms through the use of form, line and color. The clearest instance of this is Cubist art in which the artist attempt to convey on the two dimensional canvas the complexity of experience by means of a interplay of line and shading.

The next question to consider is why the brain evolved to possess such tendencies and capacities. What was the function of art in creating these special opportunities for powerful, ideal forms of human subjective experience? And most importantly, what was the evolutionary reason for the development of Art.

Neurologist Erich Harth offers an explanation for why art developed and its function in the evolution of the human brain. Harth argues that the origin of art was the same as that of language: the human brain had evolved such an ability and capacity for cognition and various levels of memory that there was a need for thinking to be aided by special symbolizing functions. In particular Harth points out the tension between new perceptions and the memory-based images that are structured into the brain – in many instances what the brain wants to see, or thinks it should see – powerfully influences what a person believes he or she perceives. In this process internal fantasies and external realities interpenetrate and co-construct.

> Artistic expression and language arise in a natural way from cognitive processes that are traceable to early primate evolution. A common characteristic of these is the formation of quasi-sensory images, so called *mental* images, under control by prefrontal cortical structures referred to as *working memory*. Such images are of necessity fleeing and incomplete. This led to a greatly enhanced ability to "see patterns" in random configurations we encounter in the world around us. The manipulation of such *external* images came to supplement the narrow channel and ephemeral characteristics of the *sketchpad-in-the-head* and became the beginning of artistic enterprise. Both artistic expression and language are *thinking tools*, their mode of operation patterned after preexisting internal cognitive processes.
>
> (Harth, 1999: 114–115)

Harth stated this point more directly in his 1995 book, *The Creative Loop: How the Brain Makes the Mind*:

> We can now appreciate the enormous advantage humans gained when they invented (or discovered) the ability to *complete the projection*, that is, to externalize their mental images beyond the sketchpad of the LGN by creating permanent images in the world around them.
>
> (Harth, 1995: 75)

Homo sapiens began to engage in making art as a result of the expanded complexity of the frontal lobes. This more powerful neural circuitry had enormous adaptive value. In particular it allowed for the creation of mental imagery (based on perception but elaborated and structured in the mind). However, the features of selectivity and exclusivity of attention, which allows us to focus and understand specific items, also limits the range of cognitive tasks we are able to perform. In other words, flooded with "ghostly and evanescent mental imagery" (Harth, 1995: 75), we also had trouble sustaining our thought processes, or thinking about more than one thing at a time. As a result people needed to develop a means to elaborate thoughts, represent and store them externally. Memory traces, mental images, which are constructed from experience and internalized in working memory, are externalized by means of artistic expression (visual images, language, sound, sculpture). Thus the mental becomes an object of perception and manipulation. As a result internal cognitive processes interact with external meaning and imagery, and both domains are further elaborated and refined. In other words art is not just a reflection of the functioning mind, it is a way that people think, feel and imagine as well as solve problems, both in external and internal realities. In art making, the mind expands beyond the physical brain, its externalized thoughts becoming the object of its own manipulation which – somewhat paradoxically – increases its own complexity and efficiency. When this process is communicated and engaged in the mind, it becomes elaborated exponentially. In art we augment our brain power and improve our minds.

From a psychoanalytic point of view Harth's model is strikingly similar to Winnicott's notion of "potential space" which is a psychological realm between private fantasy and external reality – the domain of the symbol (both discursive and non-discursive). It is through being in the world, acting together with others, that fantasy (instinctual, unstructured and unconscious) and reality can come to be "created", given personal meaning. By means of this process, in the potential space, we both create meaning and discover ourselves. Fantasy (the only psychological reality before symbolizing) according to Winnicott is static and dissociated, cut off from living and dreaming. Fantasy cannot be "worked on" or "played with" due to being unconscious but also presymbolic and implicit. In other words Fantasy cannot be thought about until it is symbolized. However, in potential space the boundaries between inner and outer change and the person becomes the interpreter, therefore creator of his experience. Reality is interpreted in terms of fantasy and fantasy in terms of reality, using each to give meaning to the other: this potential space "a place from which to become aware" makes thinking and imagination possible and manageable.

In other words language and art make possible the emergence of the symbolizing, interpreting subject by means of a dynamic link between the physical structure and operation of the brain and the world in which we live. The production of aesthetic experience (the role of line, shape and color recognition in the activation of emotions), and the need to organize and structure perception are both embedded in the design of the brain and the process of adaptation and survival. But more importantly, art expands cognition through the construction of a transitional world of symbols, the manipulation of which allows for an enhanced capacity to think, imagine and problem solve. This externalization of the subjective also made possible a remarkable expansion of self-experience, social cognition, and culture – the self-reflective person can now "be" among others in society and creativity becomes possible. As Merlin Donald (2006) noted in the quote that began this section the production and experience of art is a meta-cognitive phenomenon which cannot be understood solely from the point of view of individual cognition, rather art is a form of mental experience that is cognition "distributed" across social networks – a cognitive collectivity or community of mind which is culture – D. W. Winnicott called this the "area of cultural experience" during which private fantasy and common property (reality) are brought into relation, generating the possibility of shared meanings and ultimately a rich, complex cultural realm. (Terrence Deacon refers to these as extra-neuronal, supra-cognitive factors (Deacon, 2006, p. 29).) The next question is how and why this collective psychological phenomenon which we call art developed. What were the adaptive advantages? How did art help individuals survive? In the next section we will review some ideas from evolutionary aesthetics, adding the dimensions of survival and adaptation to our model.

The evolutionary origins of aesthetic experience and art

A growing international and interdisciplinary research project into the evolutionary and neurobiological sources of art and aesthetic experience has resulted in important new understandings of what art is and where it came from (Dissanayake, 1988, 1992, 2000; Voland and Grammer, 2003; De Sousa, 2004; Martindale *et al.*, 2007; Redies, 2007). Many now recognize that human beings can be called *Homo aestheticus* (Dissanyake, 1992) given the important role of the arts throughout human history, but also more importantly in the central role the arts play in our psychological, social and relational lives. In crucial ways the creation and valuing of art makes us human. The following sections will review some of this new research and the implications of its findings for a new definition of art. We will begin with a foundational finding, the universality of art in human life.

Ellen Dissanayake (2008a) argued that several important facts compel us to recognize that art is not just a cultural phenomenon, but also a biologically based activity which over the past 50,000 years, had clear adaptive functions.

1. They are observable cross-culturally in members of all known societies regardless of their degree of economic or technological development.
2. Their traces are evident in our ancestral past, as we find from at least 100,000 years ago with the use of red ochre and subsequent material artifacts.
3. Their rudiments are detectable and easily fostered in the behavior of young children, as when babies and toddlers spontaneously move to music, sing along or alone, make marks, decorate their bodies and possessions, play with words, find pleasure in rhythm and rhyme, and enjoy make believe.

4. They are generally attractants and sources of pleasure, like other adaptive behaviors such as mating, parenting, resting, or being with familiars in warm and safe surroundings.
5. They occur under appropriate and adaptive conditions or circumstances – that is, they are typically about important life concerns, as in ceremonies that mark stages of life or that concern prosperity, safety and subsistence.
6. They are costly: large amounts of time, physical and psychological effort, thought and material resources are devoted to the arts as to other biologically important activities (Dissanayake, 2008a).

Dissanayake explains that art can't simply be considered an accident, or an adaptive bi-product, or an incidental, pleasant form of commerce or entertainment. She believed that art has been too important for too long to too many people to not have a strong biological, adaptive source. Throughout many papers and books Dissanayake has elaborated an evolutionary model of art and aesthetic experience.

In her chapter "The arts after Darwin: Does art have an origin and adaptive function?" Dissanayake (2008b) summarized some of the claims made regarding the adaptive function of the arts. The first she lists is the idea that the arts contribute to improved problem solving and better adaptive choices. This would mean that the arts developed as a means to encode certain habitat choices, preferred sexual partners, and/or other options that might improve survival for individuals and groups. Recently research such as Christoph Redies' hypothesizes that the adaptation of visual systems to preferred natural scenes has resulted in a link between aesthetic experience and neural function. According to Redies art making is a skilled process whereby the artist unconsciously reproduces "fractal-like structures of many signals in the natural environment" (Redies, 2007, p. 6). In other words, art originated in experiences of preferred environments that have been neurologically encoded and reproduced in varieties of forms in art works: the pleasure that the viewer experiences is related to the visual stimulation of these preferences that are tied to need gratification and survival.

A second claim is that the arts developed and were adaptive because of the power of the arts to "manipulate, deceive, indoctrinate or control other people" (Nancy Ailen quoted by Dissanayake (2008b, p. 8). Dissanayake refers to an example offered by Powers (1999) of the use of red ochre paint used by women in Africa to deceive men into believing that they were fertile and available. Other researchers have argued that the persuasive quality of art was a means by which the artist gained an advantage over others and thus increased his own survival potential. A third related claim is that the arts promoted mating through the display of desirable qualities that denote fitness. The argument goes that an artist's motivation, ability and possession of resources that the display of art requires communicated to possible sexual partners the vitality, fitness and availability of the artist.

Finally Dissanayake discusses the claim of how "the arts enhance cooperation and contribute to social cohesion and continuity". Given that for most of human history the arts have been involved in communal activities, especially ritual and dance, this argument is that the shared experience of art clarifies group membership, the coordination of behavior and neural entrainment through rhythmic movements, as well as the clarification of kinship and "descent amity" (Kathryn Coe). She quoted Carroll (2004, p. xxii) who wrote: "The arts are indispensable for the organization of shared experience that makes cultural life possible."

In her discussion of these different claims for the evolutionary and adaptive origin of art, Dissanayake agrees that the function of art probably has included some if not all of these characteristics. However, she also notes that none of these claims helps us to identify the specific definition of art that we are looking for. In other words, there are many things that attract mates, manipulate people, increase social functioning, and help us make better decisions. Art may be one of these things, but what we really need to identify is the *"additional capacity"* that art has been selected for: what is special about art and what unique function does it serve in human evolution? In other words: "What do people do or accomplish when they make something art – when they 'artify'" (Dissanayake, 2008b, p. 14).

> The arts evolved not as stratagems for male competition (though like any other activity they can be used for such) but as physical correlates of psychological concern. The inborn rhythmic-model sensitivities of mutuality, through cultural elaborations, become adaptive means for arousing interest, riveting joint attention, synchronizing bodily rhythms and activities, conveying messages with conviction and memorability, and ultimately indoctrinating and reinforcing right attitudes and behavior.
>
> (Dissanayake, 2000, p. 139)

Dissanayake has suggested in several publications (1988, 1992, 1995) that the common denominator for the behavior of art is the quality of "making special" or "elaborating". The artist transforms an ordinary experience into something *extra-ordinary.* In other words, common behaviors or sensations are exaggerated, patterned, embellished, repeated, or otherwise emphasized and refined. One can see this in the rhythms and rhymes of words turned to poetry, the patterns and repetitions that turn speech to song, the design and color schemes that turn visual display into paintings, etc. In fact Dissanayake argued that *making special* is the defining characteristic of all art, throughout history.

But what are the sources of this human desire and need to *make things special?* Dissanayake argued that at the point in evolution when human beings began to make art, they drew on a "behavioral reservoir" of innate capacities and sensitivities that had evolved originally between adults and their babies. In fact she explained how the special communicative techniques between baby and adult function even to the present day to assist in communication, attachment, heightened emotion, shared awareness of special events and qualities of the world, and help to form the primary psychological bond that becomes the well and template of social and cultural life. Art is the elaboration and expansion of these early proto-aesthetic experiences and art's function in the adult human world to address and satisfy psychological and emotional needs: to stimulate feelings of belonging, to provide a sense of meaningfulness and cognitive order to individuals. Art does this with its special emotional force and refined formal structure. Through the arts audiences feel more unified and emotionally connected. In the end the shared experience of art, the participation in "something made special", plays an important role in sustaining psychobiological homeostasis, increasing the probability of individual survival and reproductive success as well as general fitness. Given the findings of evolutionary aesthetics, our next step in developing a comprehensive definition of art is to examine the matrix of art and aesthetic experience in the early attachment relationship, and the way in which the self, the mind, and artistic creation are interrelated.

The importance of attachment: adaptation, survival and aesthetic response

It is recognized that successful adaptive behaviors increase the survival of individuals and their communities. Among the most important of these behaviors, those associated with attachment between adult and infant is perhaps the most important element in human survival. An infant who is physically close to the parent, and who experiences strong emotional connection and clear, ongoing communication with the parent, will have a better chance of survival. In addition, it has been shown that secure attachment is necessary for healthy psychological development. Thus the quality of attachment will not only determine the proximity and availability of protection but also the successful realization of the child's full physical and psychological capabilities, and hence his survivability (assuming that a child with physical and psychological deficits is ultimately less effective, and thus more vulnerable). What goes on between adult and infant is often viewed as a type of fundamental form of interaction that affects all later behaviors and psychological states. The phenomenon of art in any given society has many sources and influences. However, the soul of art, its richest and deepest nature, can be found in the experience of early attachment relationships.

The parent-infant attachment relationship needs to be highly gratifying to each participant, and both work hard to develop, sustain and elaborate the bond, making it both more durable and responsive. The attachment bond is not neutral. It is defined by interactions, which express positive effects and expressive interactions. In particular Dissanayake argues that "baby talk" has a strong aesthetic character. This archaic "proto-aesthetic experience" is important to the quality of the mother-baby interaction and ongoing relationship.

The readiness for an aesthetic response to attachment behaviors is biologically based. Infants are born wanting certain visual, vocal, and movement behaviors. In response to the appropriate stimulus the baby spontaneously experiences the interaction according to some specific forms of aesthetic structuring that is built into the brain and evoked and organized in response to interaction with attachment figures. Dissanyake describes the aesthetics of baby talk as preverbal and archaic.

It may not even be conscious. It is also highly unstable and not fully organized cognitively. The child and parent respond to the quickly changing, responsive other. At the same time these interactions have formal structure (shape, color, rhythm, line, tone, etc.), which are affectively charged, formalized, repetitious, elaborate, and manipulated for surprise (Dissanayake, 2000). Most importantly proto-aesthetic interactions are heavily loaded with bi-directional value affects. The interaction of value affects results in value augmentation – in other words increasing excitement and positive feeling for each other.

Proto-aesthetic experiences enhance the self and the self-in-relation to the other. They are pleasurable and reinforcing. Over time proto-aesthetic experiences becomes organized and elaborated into more mature forms. Hence these early modes of experiencing do not disappear; rather they continue to make up a set of background, procedural memories that color all subsequent experiences. Thus human life acquires and retains an aesthetic dimension that, in general, is positively charged.

Importantly as the child's sensibility comes into interaction with the social world (by means of family influence, education and/or participation in culture and rituals) he or she elaborates and organizes higher level forms of aesthetic feeling into what will become mature aesthetic understanding and appreciation. In the experience of mature forms of art proto-aesthetic experience is a dimension of the person's appreciation of the artwork.

In summary, attachment is fundamental to all human relationships. Social cohesion and success as a community depend on the secure and vital linkage between people. Successful functioning of individuals and relationships depend on the psychological and interactional realization of secure attachment. Society and culture have many ways in which the vitalizing, healing and bonding power of attachment is infused into multiple components of social life. An important means by which this is accomplished is the creation, appreciation, and use of art.

Art making is a means by which the artist, through tools provided by his or her cultural surroundings, creates a special experience. In essence he attempts to partially restore some aspects of the early relational experience. He does this by ratifying the aspects of the artwork that reflect subjectivity. In other words, by means of art making he or she brings about an opportunity to capture the special qualities of self-experience and the archaic attachment bond. Engagement in art making is an important means by which the developing person intentionally brings about opportunities for aesthetic experience.

In sum, art making does several thing for the artist: (1) it enhances self-experience; (2) it restores a sense of connection to an ideal other, a special one (the art work as parent surrogate); (3) it offers an opportunity to refine the experience (art making involves perfecting and refining as an aspect of "making special"); (4) thus the work that the artist puts into the creation of the art work, augments the value that the artwork possesses, resulting in increased self-cohesion and vitality.

It is important to acknowledge that art making and artistic creativity is frequently a collaborative process. In fact it is highly probable that art had its source in communal activities such as dance, music making and other components of ritual practice. However, some researchers have shown how even modern Western artists pursue their art in close relationships where there is "a joint, passionate interest in a new problem, art form or societal challenge" (John-Steiner, 2000, p. 189). In addition these creative partners are part of a broader supportive community that involves mentors and friends, critics and managers – a "cultural organism", which David Feldman defines as "a cooperative structure that is formed and reformed in order to enhance the possibility for discovery, development, and (occasionally) optimal expression of human talents in various domains" (Feldman *et al.*, 1994). From this point of view the notion of the individual creative artist must be understood in a context of collaborative relationships and a dynamic social support within which art is made and elaborated.

In other words, for most human communities there is an investment in refining and enhancing the artwork. Talented individuals are given training and mentoring to increase their skills in making art and in creating the desired psychological and emotional opportunities that the appreciation of art offers. In art, the inchoate forms that potentially lie in proto-aesthetic experience, are elaborated, refined, and given organization and structure, as well as a place of prestige within the community. In this way the intimate and basic nature of the proto-aesthetic communion found between mother and child is elaborated into the often sophisticated and rarified art forms that are common to human societies.

In sum, art-making has clear adaptive value, given the powerful impact it can have on the quality of self-experience, social relations and communal integrity and vitality. Most importantly art infuses culture with the affective charge of secure attachment – it helps to provide the experience of relationships in a community with a feeling of security and affective resonance. A society that utilizes art making throughout the community and in response to many different events tend to be well functioning and effective. Its members tend to have a greater probability of survival. Relationships that share the enjoyment and/or creation of art tend to be more stable, vital and creative – also enhancing survival. Finally individuals who enjoy making art tend to be better integrated into the community, receive admiration and support from others, and enjoy a higher quality of self-experience.

References

Ansburg, P. I. and Hill, K. (2003). Affect and the therapeutic action in psychoanalysis. *International Journal of Psychoanalysis*, 86, 677–697.
Arieti, S. (1976). *Creativity: The Magic Synthesis*. New York: Basic Books.
Aron, L. and Harris, A. (Eds) (2013). *Relational Psychoanalysis: Innovation and Expansion*. Hillsdale, NJ: The Analytic Press.
Beebe, B. and Lachmann, F. (2002). *Infant Research and Adult Treatment: Co-Constructing Interactions*. Hillsdale, NJ: The Analytic Press.
Benjamin, J. (2004). Beyond doer and done to: An intersubjective view of thirdness. *The Psychoanalytic Quarterly*, 73 (1), 5–46.
Bergin, A. E. and Garfield, S. L. (1994). Overview, trends, and future issues. In A. E. Bergin and S. L. Garfield (Eds), *Handbook of Psychotherapy and Behavior Change* (4th. edn, pp. 821–830). New York: Wiley.
Bion, W. (1961). *Experience in Groups*. London: Karnac.
Bohart, A. and Tallman, K. (2003). *How Clients Make Therapy Work: The Process of Creative Self-Healing*. Washington, DC: American Psychological Association.
Boston Change Process Study Group (2005). The "something more" than interpretation revisited: Sloppiness and co-creativity in the psychoanalytic encounter. *Journal of the American Psychoanalytic Association*, 53 (3), 693–729.
Boston Change Process Study Group (2010). *Change in Psychotherapy: A Unifying Paradigm*. New York: Norton.
Bromberg, P. (1998). *Standing in the Spaces: Essays on Clinical Process*. Hillsdale, NJ: The Analytic Press.
Bromberg, P. (2006). *Awakening the Dreamer: Clinical Journeys*. Mahwah, NJ: The Analytic Press.
Brown, S. and Dissanayake, E. (2009). The arts are more than aesthetics: Neuroesthetics as narrow aesthetics. In M. Skov and O. Vartanian (Eds), *Neuroesthetics*. Amityville, NY: Baywood Publishing, pp. 43–57.
Carroll, N. (2004). Art and human nature. *The Journal of Aesthetics and Art Criticism*, 62 (2), 95–107.
Coburn, W. (2007). Psychoanalytic complexity: Pouring new wine directly into one's mouth. In P. Buirski and A. Kottler (Eds), *New Developments in Self Psychology Practice*. New York: Aronson, pp. 3–22.
Coburn, W. (2009). *Beyond Postmodernism: New Directions in Clinical Theory and practice*. New York and London: Routledge.
Danto, A. (2013). *What Art Is*. New Haven, CT: Yale University Press.

Deacon, T. (2006). The aesthetic faculty. In M. Turner (Ed.), *The Artful Mind: Cognitive Science and the Riddle of Human Creativity.* Oxford: Oxford University Press, pp. 21–53.

De Dreu, C., Nijstad, B. A., Bass, M., Wolsink, I., and Roskes, M. (2012). Working memory benefits, creative insight, musical improvisation, and original ideation through maintained task-focused attention. *Social Psychology Bulletin*, 38 (5), 656–669.

De Sousa, R. (2004). Is art an adaptation? Prospects for an evolutionary perspective on beauty. *The Journal of Aesthetics and Art Criticism*, 62 (2), 109–118.

Dissanayake, E. (1988). *What is Art for?* Seattle, WA: University of Washington Press.

Dissanayake, E. (1992). *Homo Astheticus: Where Art Comes from and Why*. New York: Free Press.

Dissanayake, E. (2000). *Art and Intimacy*. Seattle, WA: University of Washington Press.

Dissanayake, E. (2006). Fons et origo: A Darwinian view of selfobject theory and the arts. *Psychoanalytic Inquiry*, 26 (3), 309–325.

Dissanayake, E. (2008a). If music is the food of love, what about survival and reproductive success? *Musicae Scientiae, Special Issue*, 169–195.

Dissanayake, E. (2008b). The arts after Darwin: Does art have an origin and adaptive function? In K. Zijlmans and W. van Damme (Eds), *World Art Studies: Exploring Concepts and Approaches*. Amsterdam: Valiz.

Dissanayake, E. (2009). The artification hypothesis and its relevance to cognitive science, evolutionary aesthetics, and neuroaesthetics. Special Issue on Aesthetic Cognition. *Cognitive Semiotics*, 5, 148–173.

Donald, M. (2006). Art and cognition. In M. Turner (Ed.), *The Artful Mind: Cognitive Science and the Riddle of Human Creativity.* Oxford: Oxford University Press (pp. 3–20, 53).

Egan, J. and Kernberg, P. (1984). Pathological narcissism in childhood. *Journal of the American Psychoanalytic Association*, 32, 39–62.

Feldman, D., Csikszentmihalyi, M., and Gardner, H. (1994). *Changing the World: A Framework for the Study of Creativity.* Westport, CT: Praeger.

Fiorini, H. J. (2014). *The Creating Psyche: Theory and Practice of Tertiary Processes* (trans S. Rogers). Vitoria-Gastiez, Spain: Producciones AgrupArte.

Fonagy, P., Gergely, G., Jurist, E. and Target, M. (2003). *Affect Regulation, Metallization and the Development of the Self.* New York: Other Press.

Freud, S. (1908). Creative writers and day-dreaming. In J. Strachey (Ed. and Trans), *The Standard Edition of the Complete Psychological Works of Sigmund Freud, Vol. 9*, 1959, pp. 142–153. London: Hogarth Press.

Freud, S. (1910). Leonardo da Vinci and a memory of childhood. In J. Strachey (Ed. and Trans), *The Standard Edition of the Complete Psychological Works of Sigmund Freud, Vol. 11*, 1959, pp. 59–137. London: Hogarth Press.

Friedman, L. (1988). *The Anatomy of Psychotherapy*. Hillsdale, NJ, Analytic Press.

Glass, R. M. (2008). Psychodynamic psychotherapy and research evidence: Bambi survives Godzilla? *Journal of the American Medical Association*, 300, 1587–1589.

Hagman, G. (2000a). The creative process. In A. I. Goldberg (Ed.), *How Responsive Should We Be? Progress in Self Psychology, Volume 16.* Hillsdale, NJ: The Analytic Press, pp. 277–297.

Hagman, G. (2000b). The analyst's relation to the good. *Journal of the Academy of Psychoanalysis*, 28 (1), 63–82.

Hagman, G. (2005). The musician and the creative process. *Journal of the American Academy of Psychoanalysis and Dynamic Psychiatry*, 33 (1), 97–118.

Hagman, G. (2006). *Aesthetic Experience: Beauty, Creativity and the Search for the Ideal.* Amsterdam: Rodopi Press.

Hagman, G. (2010a). *The Artist's Mind: A Psychoanalytic Perspective on Creativity, Modern Art and Modern Artists.* London and New York: Routledge.

Hagman, G. (2010b). The active patient. Paper read at *International Conference on the Analysis of the Self*, Antalya, Turkey.

Hagman, G. and Rotenberg, C. (Eds) (2006), Art, creativity and psychoanalysis: Current perspectives. *Psychoanalytic Inquiry*, 26 (3), 309–325.

Harth, E. (1995). *The Creative Loop: How the Brain Makes the Mind.* Reading, MA: Addison-Wesley.

Harth, E. (1999). The emergence of art and language in the human brain. *Journal of Consciousness Studies*, 6 (6 and 7), 97–115.

John-Steiner, V. (2000). *Creative Collaboration.* Oxford, London and New York: Oxford University Press.

Kay, J. and Kay, R. L. (2011). Individual psychoanalytic psychotherapy. In A. Tasman, J. Kay, J. A. Lieberman, M. B. Flint, and M. Maj (Eds), *Psychiatry: 4th edition*. Chichester, England: Wiley, pp. 1851–1874.

Kindler, A. (2010). Improvisation, spontaneity and psychoanalysis. *Psychoanalytic Inquiry: Forms of Creative Expression in Psychoanalysis*.

Klein, G. (1976). *Psychoanalytic Theory.* Madison, CT: International Universities Press.

Kligerman, C. (1980). Art and the self of the artist. In A. Goldberg (Ed.), *Advances on Self Psychology*. Madison, CT: International Universities Press, pp. 383–391.

Knoblauch, S. H. (2000). *The Musical Edge of Therapeutic Dialogue*. Hillsdale, NJ: The Analytic Press.

Kohut, H. (1966). Forms and transformations of narcissism. In C. Strozier (Ed.), *Self Psychology and the Humanities*. New York: Norton, 1985, pp. 97–123.

Kohut, H. (1972). *The Analysis of the Self.* Madison, CT: International Universities Press.

Kohut, H. (1976). Creativeness, charisma, and group psychology. In C. Strozier (Ed.), *Self Psychology and the Humanities*. New York: Norton, 1985, pp. 793–843.

Kohut, H. (1977). *The Restoration of the Self.* Madison, CT: International Universities Press.

Kohut, H. (1979). The two analyses of Mr. Z. *International Journal of Psychoanalysis*, 60, 3–28.

Kohut, H. (1981/1991). On empathy. In P. H. Ornstein (Ed.), *The Search for the Self: Selected Writing of Heinz Kohut: 1978–1981, Vols 3–4*. New York: International Universities Press, pp. 525–535.

Kohut, H. (1984). *How Does Analysis Cure?* (A. Goldberg and P. E. Stepansky, Eds). Chicago, IL: University of Chicago Press.

Kohut, H. (1985). *Self Psychology and the Humanities* (C. Strozier, Ed.). New York: Norton.

Kohut, H. (1987). *The Kohut Seminars on Self Psychology and Psychotherapy with Adolescents and Young Adults* (M. Elson, Ed.). New York: Norton.

Kounios, J. and Beeman, M. (2010). The cognitive neuroscience of insight and its antecedents. In S. Kornguth, R. Steinberg, and M. D. Matthews (Eds.), *Neurocognitive and Physiological Factors During High-Tempo Operations.* Farnham: Ashgate Press.

Kris, E. (1952). *Psychoanalytic Explorations in Art.* Madison, CT: International Universities Press.

Kuspit, D. (2006). The emotional gains of aesthetic shock. In C. Rotenberg and G. Hagman (Eds) *Art, Creativity and Psychoanalysis: Current Psychoanalytic Perspectives. Psychoanalytic Inquiry*. Hillsdale, J: The Analytic Press.

Lachmann, F. (2001). Words and music. In A. Goldberg (Ed.), *The Narcissistic Patient Revisited: Progress in Self Psychology, Vol. 17*. Hillsdale, NJ: The Analytic Press, pp. 167–178.

Lachmann, F. (2004). On the co-construction of empathy. Paper delivered at the 27th Annual International Conference on the Psychology of the Self. San Diego, California.

Langer, S. (1942). *Philosophy in a New Key: A Study in the Symbolism of Reason, Rite, and Art*. Cambridge, MA: Harvard University Press.

Langer, S. (1953). *Feeling and Form*. New York: Charles Scribner's Sons.

Langer, S. (1957). *Problems of Art*. New York: Charles Scribner's Sons.

Lehrer, J. (2012). *Imagine: How Creativity Works*. New York: Houghton Mifflin.

Lichtenberg, J. (1988). Infant research and self psychology. In A. Goldberg (Ed.), *Frontiers in Self Psychology: Progress in Self Psychology, Vol. 3*. Hillsdale, NJ: The Analytic Press, pp. 59–64.

Lichtenberg, J. (1989). *Psychoanalysis and Motivation*. Hillsdale, NJ: The Analytic Press.

Lichtenberg, J. (1999). Listening, understanding and interpreting: Reflection on complexity. *International Journal of Psychoanalysis*, 80, 719–737.

Lichtenberg, J., Lachmann, F., and Fosshage, J. L. (1992). *Self and Motivational Systems. Toward a Theory of Psychoanalytic Technique*. Hillsdale, NJ: The Analytic Press.

Lichtenberg, J., Lachmann, F., and Fosshage, J. L. (1996). *The Clinical Exchange: Techniques Derived from Self and Motivational Systems*. Hillsdale, NJ: The Analytic Press.

Loewald, H. W. (1960). On the therapeutic action of psychoanalysis. *International Journal of Psycho-Analysis*, 41, 16–33.

Martindale, C., Lochner, P., and Petrov, V. M. (2007). *Evolutionary and Neurocognitive Approaches to Aesthetics, Creativity and the Arts*. Amityville, NY: Baywood.

McGilchrist, I. (2009). *The Master and His Emissary: The Divided Brain and the Making of the Modern World*. New Haven, CT: Yale University Press.

Merkin, D. (2010). My life in therapy. *New York Times*, 4 August. Available at: www.nytimes.com/2010/08/08/magazine/08Psychoanalysis-t.html

Ogden, T. (1994). The analytical third: Working with intersubjective clinical facts. *International Journal of Psychoanalysis*, 75 (1), 3–19.

Oppenheim, L. (2005). *A Curious Intimacy: Art and Neuropsychoanalysis*. London and New York: Routledge.

Phillips, A. (1998). *The Beast in the Nursery*. New York: Pantheon.

Powers, S. (1999). *The Art of Getting Over: Graffiti at the Millennium*. New York: Macmillan.

Press, C. (2002). *The Dancing Self: Creativity, Modern Dance, Self Psychology and Transformative Education*. Cresskill, NJ: Hampton Press.

Press, C. and Hagman, G. (2010). Between aesthetics: The coconstruction of empathy and the Clinical. *Psychoanalytic Inquiry*, 30 (3), 207–221.

Protter, E. (1997). *Painters on Painting*. Mineola, NY: Dover Publications.

Ramachandran, V. S. (2005). *The Artful Brain*. New York: Harper Collins.

Redies, C. (2007). A Universal model of aesthetic perception based on coding of natural stimuli. *Spatial Vision*, 21 (1 and 2), 97–117.

Renik, O. (2001). The patient's experience of therapeutic benefit. *Psychoanalytic Quarterly*, 70 (1), 231–242.

Renik, O. (2003). Standards and standardization. *Journal of the American Psychoanalytic Association*, 51, 43–55.

Ringstrom, P. (2001). Cultivating the improvisational in psychoanalysis. *Psychoanalytic Dialogue*, 11, 727–754.

Roland, A. (2003). *Drama and Delusion.* Middletown, CT: Wesleyan.

Rose, G. (1992). *The Power of Form* (Expanded Edition). New York: International Universities Press.

Rose, G. J. (2004). *Between Couch and Piano: Psychoanalysis, Music, Art and Neuroscience.* New York: Brunner-Routledge.

Rotenberg, C. (1988). Selfobject theory and the artistic process. In A. Goldberg (Ed.), *Learning from Kohut: Progress in Self Psychology, Vol. 4*. Hillsdale, NJ: The Analytic Press, pp. 193–213.

Rotenberg, C. (1992). Optimal operative perversity: A contribution to the theory of creativity. In A. Goldberg (Ed.), *New Therapeutic Visions: Progress in Self Psychology, Vol. 8*. Hillsdale, NJ: The Analytic Press, pp. 167–188.

Rothenberg, A. (1979). *The Emerging Goddess: The Creative Process in Art, Science, and Other Fields*. Chicago, IL: University of Chicago Press.

Sachs, H. (1942). *The Creative Unconscious*. Cambridge, MA: Sci-Art Publishers.

Schafer, R. (1976). *A New Language for Psychoanalysis.* New Haven, CT: Yale University Press.

Schafer, R. (1983). *The Analytic Attitude.* New York: Basic Books.

Schore, A. (1994). *Affect Regulation and the Origin of the Self.* Mahwah, NJ: Erlbaum.

Schore, A. (2003). *Affect Regulation and the Repair of the Self.* New York: Norton.

Schore, A. (2012). *The Science of the Art of Psychotherapy*. New York: Norton.

Segal, H. (1952). A psychoanalytic approach to aesthetics. *International Journal of Psychoanalysis*, 33, 196–207.

Segal, H. (1957). A psychoanalytical approach to aesthetics. In M. Klein, P. Heimann, and R. E. Money-Kyrle (Eds) *New Directions in Psychoanalysis*. New York: Basic Books, pp. 384–405.

Segal, H. (1991). *Dream, Phantasy and Art*. London: Routledge.

Seki, S. (1999). Art and the brain. *Journal of Consciousness Studies*, 6 (6–7), 76–96.

Shaddock, D. (2010). The opening of the field: Thoughts on the poetics of psychoanalytic treatment. *Psychoanalytic Inquiry: Forms of Creative Expression in Psychoanalysis*.

Shedler, J. (2010). The efficacy of psychodynamic psychotherapy. *American Psychologist*, 65, 98–109.

Slavin, M. and Kriegman, D. (1998). Why the analyst needs to change: Toward a theory of conflict, negotiation, and mutual influence in the therapeutic process. In L. Aron and A. Harris (Eds), *Relational Psychoanalysis: Innovation and Expansion.* Hillsdale, NJ: The Analytic Press, pp. 75–119.

Stern, D. B. (1997). *Unformulated Experience: From Dissociation to Imagination in Psychoanalysis.* Hillsdale, NJ: The Analytic Press.

Stern, D. N. (1985). *The Interpersonal World of the Infant: A View from Psychoanalysis and Developmental Psychology*. New York: Basic Books.

Stern, D. N. (2004). *The Present Moment in Psychotherapy and Everyday Life.* Norton: New York.

Stolorow, R. (1997). Dynamic, dyadic, intersubjective systems: An evolving paradigm for psychoanalysis. *Psychoanalytic Psychology*, 14 (3), 337–364.

Stolorow, R. (2007). *Trauma and Human Existence.* Hillsdale, NJ: The Analytic Press.

Stolorow, R. and Atwood, G. (1992). *Contexts of Being: The Intersubjective Foundations of Psychological Life.* Hillsdale, NJ: The Analytic Press.

Summers, F. (2005). *Self Creation: Psychoanalytic Therapy and the Art of the Possible.* Analytic Press: Hillsdale, NJ.

Tolpin, M. (1997). Compensatory structures: Paths to restoration. In A. Goldberg (Ed.), *Conversations in Self Psychology: Progress in Self Psychology*, Vol. 13. Hillsdale, NJ: The Analytic Press, pp. 3–19.

Tolpin, M. (1997). *Compensatory Structures: Paths to the Restoration of the Self, Progress in Self Psychology.* Mahwah, NJ: Analytic Press.

Tolpin, M. (2002). Doing psychoanalysis of normal development: Forward edge transferences. In A. Goldberg (Ed.), *Postmodern Self Psychology: Progress in Self Psychology*, Vol. 18. Hillsdale, NJ: The Analytic Press, pp. 167–190.

Voland, E. and Grammer, K. (2003). *Evolutionary Aesthetics.* New York and Heidelberg: Springer.

Weiss, J. (1994). The analyst's task: To help the patient carry out his plan. *Contemporary Psychoanalysis*, 30, 236–254.

Weiss, J. (1998). Patients' unconscious plans for solving their problems. *Psychoanalytic Dialogues*, 8, 411–428.

Weiss, J. and Sampson, H. (1986). *The Psychoanalytic Process: Theory, Clinical Observation and Empirical Research.* New York: Guilford.

Wiley, J. and Jarosz, A.F. (2012). Working memory capacity, attentional focus, and problem solving. *Current Directions in Psychological Science*, 21 (4), 258–262.

Winnicott, C., Shepherd, R. and Winnicott, D. W. (1971). *Playing and Reality*. New York: Basic Books.

Winnicott, D. W. (1970). *Home is Where We Start From.* Harmonsworth: Penguin.

Winnicott, D.W. (1971). *Therapeutic Consultations in Child Psychiatry.* New York: Basic Books.

Zeki, S. (2000). *Inner Vision: An Exploration of Art and the Brain.* New York and Oxford: Oxford University Press.

Index